W9-BDL-965

Central Skagit Sedro-Woolley Library
802 Ball St.
Sedro-Woolley WA 98284
Oct 2019

This is a work of nonfiction. These stories are told the way I remember them, not necessarily how others do. Some names and identifying details have been changed.

Copyright © 2018
Natalie Singer

All rights reserved. No part
of this book may be repro-
duced in any form or by any
electronic or mechanical
means, including informa-
tion storage-and-retrieval
systems, without prior permission in writing from the
Publisher, except for brief
quotations embodied in
critical articles and reviews.

Library of Congress
Cataloging-in-Publication Data

Names:
Singer, Natalie, 1977– author.

Title:
California calling : a self interrogation /
by Natalie Singer.

Description:
Portland, Oregon : Hawthorne Books,
2015.

Identifiers:
LCCN 2017015665
ISBN 9780998825717 (print)
ISBN 9780998825724 (digital)

Subjects:
LCSH: Singer, Natalie, 1977– | Young
women—California—Biography. | Cana-
dians—California—Biography. | Coming
of age. | Man-woman relationships. | Cal-
ifornia—Social life and customs.

Classification:
LCC CT3262.C25 S56 2015
DDC 979.4/054092 [B] —dc23

LC record available at
https://lccn.loc.gov/2017015665

Hawthorne Books
& Literary Arts

9 2201 Northeast 23rd Avenue
8 3rd Floor
7 Portland, Oregon 97212
6 hawthornebooks.com
5 Form:
4 Sibley House
3
2 Printed in China

Set in Kingfisher

For Lukas

CALIFORNIA CALLING

A SELF-INTERROGATION

NATALIE SINGER

 HAWTHORNE BOOKS & LITERARY ARTS
Portland, Oregon | MMXVII

Contents

CALIFORNIA CALLING

The people who stayed behind and had their settled ways—those people were not the people who got the prize. The prize was California.

—JOAN DIDION

Prologue

I AM IN A COURTROOM. THE COLOR PALETTE IS CREAMY SHELLS and brass, cold emerald lawyers' lamps and spit-polished mahoganies. I am in the corner in a witness box. The audience stares at me hard. I have been put here to testify about what it is to be female, a sister, a mother (though I am not a mother, I am a sixteen-year-old girl). To testify about adultery. I am asked who I am. What I am. Who we have allowed inside of us. I must defend the women in my family, all the way back, and every girl and woman who ever was. Something fundamental is breaking and I will be responsible. The black veins of the marble floor look like cheese mold, cords of rot. I open my lips and out comes…vapor.

PART ONE

Formation

Formation

THERE ARE FOUR STAGES OF INTERROGATION; THE FIRST IS CALLED
Formation. Before the interrogation comes the need for it to occur and the
mandate to undertake it. At this stage, the framework is established for
how the interrogation may be determined, including the level of coercion
that is permitted or not allowed.

What happened in the library?

My affair with California begins long before we meet.

I am nine, tucked between stacks in the school library on the second floor. For years after, decades, I will have dreams about the second floor of this school. I will wrestle in my sleep to remember what the hallway looked like as it hooked a sharp right, to the farthest reaches of the building where only the sixth-graders went. I will smell the disinfectant wafting off the floors and hear the squeak of untied sneakers. I will remember, without knowing if it is real, a tide of anxiety about the girls' bathroom—dirty stalls, cold tile, donut-shaped communal drinking fountain into which one could easily fall, or be pushed.

But the library is safe. I run my hand over the familiar rows of soft weathered spines, some torn fuzzily. The books have a certain smell: musty, the way I think the insides of the ancient mummy sarcophagi we learned about in class would smell if they were pried open.

I have a research project, assigned by Madame Sebag, who hates me and forces me to copy French dictionary pages when I forget to have my parents sign my homework, which is all the time. The research project must be on a country in the world, any country other than Canada, our own. It is due in three weeks. I am pulsing with excitement. I am in the fourth grade. I want to pick a rad country, one no one else will have. Madame Sebag will see how good I am.

The geography section is pretty decent, six shelves. The winter sun glints from the high-up rectangle windows, lighting the dust flakes in the air that look like goldfish food and the shiny plants our librarian, who wears stiff brown pantsuits and orange-flowered blouses, keeps on the top shelves. I see a book, *All About California*.

I open it.

As part of the Pacific Ring of Fire, California is subject to tsunamis, floods, drought, Santa Ana winds, landslides, wildfires, and has several volcanoes. It has numerous earthquakes, in particular along the San Andreas Fault....

Death Valley, a desert with large expanses below sea level, is the hottest place in North America; the highest temperature in the Western Hemisphere, 134° F (57° C), was recorded there July 10, 1913....

The name California is believed to have derived from a fictional paradise populated by black women warriors and ruled by Queen Calafia...a remote land also inhabited by man-eating griffins and other strange mythical beasts, and rich in gold.

I try to mentally X-ray the pictures of spiky palm trees, blood-red underground faults, nuggets of gold, soaring ocean waves, and sidewalk stars engraved with famous actresses' names. I stare these pages down, bore into them. Hollywood stars on the sidewalk—ohmygod maybe Molly Ringwald is there, and Alyssa Milano, and Drew Barrymore from *E.T.*

Already my mind is engulfed by California. Forget the project for horrible Madame Sebag. Forget Lake Placid, where my parents take us to stay in my grandparents' vacation cabin every summer—I want to go to California.

How can I get there? Maybe if I do a totally awesome project my parents will decide we can go to California for a visit. Maybe they will know immediately that we all belong there; maybe they will love it as much as I do. Maybe California will help them love each other.

I look back at *All About California*, hungry for more inspiration.

"California is the 3rd largest state in the United States in size, after Alaska and Texas."

A state? A *state*? Like New York, where we drive once a year across the border to do our school shopping, hiding new clothes and shoes deep in our Jeep's trunk on our way back, away from the customs officials so we don't have to pay extra taxes?

Slowly I put the book back on its shelf. The library wall clock reads 3:58. In two minutes my mom will be outside in the car to pick me up.

I skim the shelves again and see *All About Italy*. Fine, whatever. I scrawl my name at the bottom of the card on the inside of the cover to check it out. Hitching my heavy winter coat tightly around me, I step down the stairs and out into the snow.

Affair might be too strong a word

Not too strong. Too strange? I am writing about becoming obsessed with a state. A state of the U. S. Can you stalk a state? A state of being, yes. A state of becoming. A state of belonging, of trying to belong. The thirty-first state. First state I love. The state of love.

State your purpose

I'm trying.

So this is a love story?

It is about how we search for things we don't know are there, bringing myths to life. It is about longing. The taste of it and the shame of it. It is about mapping one's way out of the silence of girlhood.

It is not a love story about California. It is a love story with California.

We should talk about form

I have a relationship with interrogation. A trio of memories, a history bequeathed. This has everything to do with searching. The first memory of interrogation, the foundation of my form of inquiry, went down long before I was born.

My family's roots reach back to Russia, to days of overwhelming love and fear. In the early twentieth century, they planned their escape from the shtetls, their small Jewish towns where the pillagers came again and again and the parents hid their beautiful daughters beneath the floorboards. Steam trunks were packed: hand-sewn linens; precious dishes; the books that held their past and futures; the babies—always such care with the babies. Enough money saved to afford second-class passage, then maybe a hard end of bread when they landed.

When they arrived from the shtetl to the city of Odessa, their turn at interrogation neared. They had readied their aging parents, studied the documents, rehearsed what to say. Know enough about where you want to go, but not too much. Respect your oppressors, but never sarcastically. Admit that the only home you have ever known is for the others, or if necessary (and it will be necessary) that you are the other. Speak but do not speak. Say the right thing. Reshape your story into a version attested to, a version to satisfy those in power—this is what it takes to obtain passage, to be given a chance at life. To avoid, now and later, the butts of guns, the bullets of guns, the pits, the gas, the ovens. To be allowed to continue the family. Such an essential thing: to continue to unspool one's thread.

The day came, a long line of waiting, worrying. Fold, open, read, refold your papers. Hush your children. Wring hands. Think hate; hurriedly subdue it. When my family arrived at the front of the line, the inquisition moved swiftly, faster than they'd thought, catching them in its current, steering their stories away from them. Where are you going? Why are you going? What will you do what have you done who do you know?

How they answered, it turned out, mattered not much at all. After all that rehearsing, it turned out one of them, the grandmother, had an eye infection. Passage out of the place that did not want them was refused. Their declaration denied, their requests silenced. File closed.

Until

If

Just maybe . . .

Tickets for second-class passage, it turned out, could be sold to pay for a year of life-or-death survival in Odessa.

It turned out, after one year of uncertainty, of squeaking by, of keeping quiet, of trying again, giving the right answers, brightening that old eye, being happy with steerage, miracle of miracles, they got out.

What other legacy was bequeathed?

One branch bore five siblings, four brothers and a girl. They were given passage, would survive the boat. On board the sister was often missing, alone in her dreams they figured. Thinking her stories. They disembarked to a new white north, cobbled streets and crowded walkups, a blank page on which to write their destinies. But before they even settled, before the boys had forged business from their guts and gumption, before they made love to a new language with their tongues, she was gone. It was rumored she had run off with a Russian soldier, the objective correlative for their instigating sorrow. Everyone talks. Instantly they released her, my mother's scandalous ancestor. She was dead to them, having chosen pleasure over duty, never to be seen or spoken of again.

But they did speak of her, some of the brothers, and tried later to find her. They could not, which left some of the men with a bothersome sentiment, and all the girls who came after with a tremor in their cells.

Will I always remember California?

You can trace the spine of a state. Trace a line south from the hollow of her neck down along her vertebrae, from wet hills to rough mountains to reckless caverns dripping in the middle heady like verdant jungles, like the misted tropics they are, course along vertiginous roads that are cliffs to milkshake rivers below, gush with fossil-mud, with leftover dreamed-of gold, with rockslides crowned in fog, dodge prehistoric pinecones the size of footballs and the weight of watermelons, seed-sodden and slimy, alive in your hands.

You can trace this spine along sandy banks and red-and-black mineral-striped earth, knolls like the rolling hips of women through freeway knots and pastel beach towns and strip malls that blur into one another and low-slung fruit-packing plants and Art Deco marquees on main streets dead and gasping and queues of orange trees heavy with reward. You can push your way through the tip of the desert, blurry at the edges, past dusty antique shops, shell-shocked desert huts and counter-culture dome homes, matchstick palms leaning into each other for company and anchoring you always to the here even as it changes and changes and changes.

I do not need coercing

affirm   attest   disclose   confess   concede

   come clean   divulge

                yield

declare

                           swear
                  surrender

                              release

                     State.

PART TWO

Preparation

Preparation

BEFORE THE INTERROGATOR MOVES INTO ACTION, A FURTHER preparation is often appropriate in which he will learn the facts of the case, the desired outcome, and the constraints of the permitted process.

  This then leads to appropriate research and preparation of methods and techniques that the interrogator will use. As the person being questioned may successfully resist some approaches, multiple strategies and tactics may be readied.

Identify the point of departure

1993

The beginning of the end of this family was the moment we all filed down the accordion walkway and onto the crammed, sunset-bound 747. By boarding this plane, we sealed our fate.

We sat hip to hip in one long row, the seven of us unbroken in line but barely believable as a family unit. For one thing, we didn't look at all like each other, which makes sense: among the five kids, we sprung from three different fathers and two different mothers.

In case of an emergency, please secure the air mask to yourself before helping others, instructed the Air Canada flight attendant.

In case of an emergency, which family members would I rush to save and which would I not bother with?

Steven, my still-cherubic eleven-year-old brother, slipped on his headphones and punched at a video game. Zachary, six, adjusted his baseball cap over his golden head and launched a pair of plastic Ninja Turtles into battle. They were okay, I thought. Sometimes annoying, but, still, my real siblings, the blood relations, worth keeping.

Next sat my mother, then me, joined together by nerves. We were leaving our hometown, possibly forever. We were going somewhere inconceivably big, and it still seemed so impossible that occasionally we whispered the word to ourselves under our gum-freshened breath: California. Land of sunshine and Hollywood mansions, palm trees and rippling American flags. We were going to the West, the farthest west we could go from where we were—the unpredictable rim of the continent and the edge of what our imaginations could conjure. All we had for reference were *Cosmo* and *Vogue* magazines, which told us what we'd need to wear and buy and consume to become American women, and our memorized episodes of Beverly Hills 90210.

If there was a soundtrack for our leaving, it was Zeppelin's "Going to California." I ran it in a loop through my head. I was going to California, an aching in my heart.

I tried not to think of what was being left.

I looked out the airplane window: gray industrial buildings, the smoggy Montreal summer air hanging in a thick yellow belt, and, obscured by the drabness, the stultified suburbs of both my childhood and my mother's.

Are you okay, my mom asked me. She wrung her hands in her lap, those slender fingers, gold bracelets clicking. I nodded, drawing down a veil with my long hair, and swallowed the puddle in my throat.

From the end of the airplane row came Josef's booming voice, his thick Israeli accent curling the Rs at the beginning of words and dropping them in the middle, turning the heads of strangers compelled to investigate Middle Eastern-sounding foreigners in their midst.

Rrrready? my step-father asked us. Ready for the adventure of a lifetime? California here we come! He sounded like Arnold Schwarzenegger in a tourist board commercial, years before the Terminator would be reborn into a politician. By then California would have written its story all over us.

None of the boys looked up from their toys. I rolled my eyes, and my mother and I both nodded quickly. Please, I knew she was thinking, like I was, stop talking to us.

The airplane lurched and roared. I glanced sideways at the others. Josef's shiny head was now bent over the science and engineering magazines in his lap. Next to him was Ric, my thirteen-year-old step-brother, his dark brow furrowed, thumbs racing over the buttons of a handheld game.

Beside Ric was Asher, bony with skin so pale it was an otherworldly milk-glass bluish. Josef's other son, sixteen—my age. Most likely it was Nirvana in his earphones. He refused to look up at anyone; later, when the stewardess asked if he'd like a drink, he answered with his eyes to the ground.

I understood that tragedy had rendered Asher broken with

uncertain hope of repair. I stared for a second before glancing away. Eye contact with Asher had to be avoided at all costs. We were all sad, but he was the saddest.

The seven of us were a hastily and sloppily assembled family, like a project for the school science fair. From afar we might have looked fine, natural, but up close globs of glue seeped out from misaligned corners, popsicle sticks were crooked; the whole thing could topple with the flick of a finger or a puff of wind. The materials used to construct our family were off-brand, heavy with the industrial scent of after-market problems: death, betrayal, shame, abandonment.

We were the Brady Bunch minus the upbeat tempo, conspicuously second-chance, step-family awkward. We were all searching for something, but we didn't quite know what. If we had known, I don't think we'd have told each other.

But I didn't care. None of us did. What we were heading toward was bigger than a natural, perfect family. In that plane, over the next six hours, I would cross over into what I hoped would be my own version of freedom. By the time the plane touched down at the San Jose International Airport, I would be unburdened of the pressures of my old high school, the weight of family secrets that burned like a brand, and the loneliness of my existence in the nowhere of the North.

Something was calling to me.

California.

What do you think California will be like?

It will be like a secret society.
Like pineapple Jell-O.
Frangelico cream.
It will be like a woman in a silver Speedo and an alligator mask.
Shaving her legs in a public fountain.
A jar of marmalade.
A pink tattoo.
A Barbie doll with hair you can braid.
It will be like a silk nightgown a baby bear tongue-tied nightingale a wet
       nurse laurel shrine sugar pine larkspur revolt a quiet scream.
It will be like a dream.

Begin in the solace

1980

There are other childhood images in my mind, from before the school library, when I am three and four. My parents and I live, for a brief opening, in Florida. Carefree. An exodus from the claustrophobic island of Montreal to which our families had been anchored for about seventy-five years, since that escape from Russia. We are imposters, not really Floridians or Americans. But we pass, or we divert ourselves with the pleasure of trying.

The memories are all set to music, a dreamy, hazy seventies sitcom-scape. We are *Three's Company* but the family version. The palette is golden, dusty oranges, brown plaids, many sun-fractured yellows. The things that are most important to us are fresh orange juice, sunbathing, going to Red Lobster to suck buttered crustaceans, cruising town in our wood-paneled station wagon, and my father's record player. It is just the three of us, and three is a magic number. On hot nights I shimmy out of my bed and my father and mother lounge around the living room on the brown nubby couch in their terry cloth shorts drinking Coca-Cola. They place my father's giant black headphones comically over my frizzy hair and eager ears and hand me a microphone. I belt out Beach Boys or Bee Gees and twirl in my Strawberry Shortcake nightgown while the skinny palms sweat the night away outside.

We listen to whatever my father has in his collection, which includes Bruce Springsteen calling everybody out for having a hungry heart; the Eagles forecasting a heartache tonight; and Gloria Gaynor promising she will survive. The Mamas & the Papas; Sonny & Cher; Jefferson Airplane; Fleetwood Mac: we sing along even though none of us can carry a tune. We speak against the backdrop of this music, this California sound, this fantasy.

The music sounds like summer nights, cotton candy, roller skates on blacktop; it reminds me of when the tide is high and that we are family, and it also makes me wonder what exactly is a hot child in the city? It is black afros and white afros and sunglasses and disco balls and chocolate milkshakes and drive-ins and my once-fifteen-year-old mother's dried school-dance corsage preserved in her special memory trunk and rounded-block fonts and tight-ass Sassons and my dad's baby blue wedding tuxedo and triangle bikinis and trips to my favorite place on Earth, Disney World, where at the petting zoo I touch a deer and in the sepia-toned picture that results and forms the memory forever, the bright white of my jeans is mirrored in the spots on the deer's tail.

Music sings through car speakers: my mom's long, low, wood-paneled station wagon as we cruise the Publix parking lot; my dad's doorless, bird-blue Jeep CJ, bumping my tiny butt to nursery school.

Saturday is *American Bandstand*, and we're free of any responsibilities. My parents are only in their twenties; their parents and siblings and most of their friends are back in the cold North. We all gather around the TV with our OJ, Daddy in his Jew 'fro and brown Top-Siders and pink Lacoste polo and Mummy in a long, mustard-colored jersey dress, slender and sunburned. Dick Clark comes on in his own pink shirt, and the dancers, young and cool like my parents, crowd the California stage. They boogie on and on.

Which things last?

Memory is funny that way. One sniff, one note, and the whole lost world opens up again.

Later, much later and no matter where I am, but especially as I cruise the California highways with the radio blaring, I will always be able to conjure the packed dance floor of *American Bandstand* on our TV screen. I will remember the embers of my parents' Marlboros tapped into tiger's eye ashtrays; the spray of surf; my mother's Chanel perfume and pink Bublicious chewing gum and lemony Mr. Clean and her hidden, hungry heart.

Tell a story about night

It was hot and sticky. From the east, a swamp wind wafted, carrying the pucker of alligator sweat. The moon was full and high outside the open window, and the little girl watched it from her narrow bed, a thin coverlet pulled up to her nose. Each night her parents would tuck her in.

"Sleep tight, don't let anything bite," said her mother, her shiny red nails sweeping the dark curls aside so she could kiss the child's soft white cheek.

"Sleep tight, don't let anything bite," said her father, pinching her playfully on the derriere.

"Tomorrow is Saturday," the mother added. "Your father doesn't have to go off to work. Don't wake us up early."

The door was closed behind the parents. Tonight was the night for her plan. The girl was four. She shivered in her thin eyelet nightgown despite the day's heat rising from the cul-de-sac's blacktop and from deep inside the creases of the palm trees. Outside a bullfrog let go its rubber croak; another answered it.

The girl closed her eyes. First the black of her eyelids was all there was, empty, not what she wanted. Under the coverlet she balled her tiny fists and began to chant as she had practiced. "I want to see you, I want to see you, I want to see you," she mumbled, her lips moving softly.

Nothing. The girl squeezed harder, and let her mind wander to the original source of her obsession. She had seen her many times, the last of which was a few days ago, projected on the TV screen in the hours of a sultry afternoon after she had returned home from preschool. And again before that, turning the well-worn pages of her faithful picture book. It took a long time for her to appear in the story—Snow White had to be mistreated, then flee, befriend the small forest men, and spy her beloved from afar. It was worth the wait, though, the girl thought, another shiver slipping underneath her gown like ice on the back of her sweaty knees.

She would conjure her, she would. "I want to see you, I want to see you, I want to see you," she whispered, louder this time. She stilled her body in wait. "I'm not afraid." *Come on. Come on.*

Nothing. She turned and opened her heavy eyes to the window. A silver tendril floated across the moon. A cricket shifted its wings. The toads sang their chorus. The girl looked back across her room and her eyes caught on something in her vanity mirror. Slowly, a wicked dark shape came into focus. The little girl sucked in her breath. It was the reflection of something, someone, up high in the corner near the ceiling. She arched her neck off the sheet to look.

A most wretched face stared down at her, more horrid than the pages of her book, than the Disney movie, than anything in her imagination. Crumpled gray skin, a sharply hooked nose, a crone's body draped in blanket rags and bent over a dead staff. Eyes that reached out and shook her to her bones, a wide, glassy stare, a band of red burning around the stone-black pupil. The warty mouth stretched slowly into a toothless grin, and a cackle came up from deep inside her body.

I will not scream, I will not scream, the little girl thought. I made her come. I'm not afraid.

But she was afraid. The old witch's arm reached out from the corner of the ceiling where she floated. She will snatch me, she will snatch me away. Yet the girl was frozen there, unable to move, unable to conjure her voice now that she wanted it most of all. Caught in the throat of herself. The witch dislodged from the ceiling, grew larger and larger, moved closer and closer, her cackle now a shriek that made the turtles turn over in the slough. The girl squeezed her eyelids shut, her mouth stuck, as a bony hand encircled her waist. I should never have asked, I should never have asked.

And another one

On a steamy Florida evening as I lie in bed in my cotton nightgown, I catch sight out the window of my father, sitting in the backyard, cigarette smoke rising in the dusk. His head bobs up and down the way it does when he listens to the Beach Boys. I creep to my window.

My blue and white metal swing set, aglow now in the early night, is my favorite thing. Every day I ride its slide and seats and climb its bars. I have never thought about what its cool poles and rocking motions might be like in the mystery of nighttime, beyond my usual bounds of play.

My father calls me softly by my nickname, Nou, like a question. And suddenly he is lifting me carefully, magically, through the open window and into the yard. My mother, probably washing dishes or reading Danielle Steel, would never let me out so late, and the shock of this fast-evolving secret—me flying through a nighttime window and into the familiar yet strange yard—electrifies me.

Lifted. Blades of grass caress my feet. I can smell the ocean. My curly hair, thick and moist and too heavy for a four-year-old's head, frizzes extra at the wall of heat outside. Frogs that suction to the side of our stucco house on hot nights burp their low croaks. My dad's face is lobster red, the flush of my parents' sun worship; it radiates against his dark curls and white polo, tight on his lanky frame.

My father, winking at me, lowers me onto the swing, pulls back, then releases me. I pump my skinny legs higher against the sky and watch the twinkling stars slide out from behind the swirls of smoke.

You're not saying anything about your mother

Right. Oversight, sorry. Because she is everywhere, everything, rule arbiter and family concierge and friend of my days, every minute of them. Every couple of mornings we go together to get a jug of orange juice from a store with flat blue carpet that also sells, of all things, rotisserie chicken. Sweet juice and chicken, enough to live off indefinitely on a peninsula all our own. She needlepoints, flowered pillows and slightly psychedelic abstracts. She went to art school for a little while. We feed ducks at a pond: in the picture she is crouched, her tanned skinny legs folded easily beneath her, a brown terry cloth jumper with short shorts, Farah Fawcett hair flipped brightly. White teeth, claret lips, the aura of her directed watchfully out of the frame toward a toddling me, chasing feathers.

Do men look at her? I don't know. Yes. My father does, smacks her ass, teasingly calls her *mieskeit*, Yiddish for ugly, which is the opposite.

Where are you really from?

1987

I'm ten now. We're back from Florida, settled in our Canadian suburb. We are still a normal family, with a tine-marked kitchen table, maple leaves piled in the backyard, car washes on the weekend. Dinners with grandparents, aunts, uncles. My parents have a set of rainbow sheets, so soft after a thousand washes their cotton against my cheek feels like silk.

There are five people now in my family: my parents, my five-year-old brother, our newborn baby brother, and me. We hang in a portrait on the wall. My father, dark hair and a camel-hair suit; my mother, pretty in chiffon; me, angelically gap-toothed in a dress that twirls wildly when I dance; my brother, in dimples; and the baby, perched in my mother's arms— the only blond except for her (but hers is from a box). The picture is from a wedding we attended, but we dance at home, too, to the new records my father buys sometimes, Michael Jackson, Madonna, Prince, Eurhythmics.

I like two boys at school, both named Darrell but one is spelled Daryl. Sometimes on the weekend I come up with the idea for a self-improvement project. For instance, organizing my wardrobe, in which I try to match new outfits that will make me look extra pretty, grown up, popular. I haven't started to develop yet, but this summer my mother has given me a tube of white powdery balm and told me I need to apply it to my armpits every morning. So insulting, I think. But this pointed, specific shame eventually blends in with my overall suspicions about growing up. Sometimes I sniff myself or examine the crevices, new tender curves, and old bicycle-bruised planes of my girl's body in the bathtub, searching for any betrayal, clues of what is to come. It feels as if, at any moment, some change will occur that I will not be able to undo.

At night I pretend my canopy bed is a ship out to sea and that my stuffed animals and I are the only ones aboard. The risk is pirates but they never come near, though sometimes I wake up in the middle of the night on my carpeted floor. One night I leave my room in a walking sleep; my father catches me just as I place my foot at the top of the stairs. Another night from my bed I hear my parents, who are just on the other side of the wall: The same goddamn thing all the time, not like I've ever had a choice, watch it.

My school is nearby. This year we discover how to dye the snow with drops of fruit punch we conserve from our lunches and mix with water from the drinking fountain. Overnight the tinted snow freezes and the next day we find glittering ice castles in its place, magenta, persimmon, amethyst. In our mittens and hats we build up our castles and watch from the schoolyard for black vans that might lead to our kidnapping. We have learned from TV news reports about children swiped off sidewalks, sold, locked away, buried. We have heard from our parents about six-year-old Etan Patz, who disappeared from his Manhattan neighborhood while walking the few blocks to the bus stop. Strangers mean danger. Any van turning the corner creates ripples of panic among the children behind the playground's chain-link fence. Sometimes I think about what happens to you in a kidnapping, news headlines of CHILD SEX RINGS and TEEN PREGNANCY EPIDEMIC and SERIAL RAPIST LOOSE in my mind. In my irridescent pink Hello Kitty journal I write about how I hope I will never be grabbed and stolen and bound and worse, whatever worse is; I pray I will never need to kick out the brake light from the inside of a darkened trunk to save myself from a fat man in a leather motorcycle vest. I rehearse the investigative and escape skills I have gleaned from reading Nancy Drew and watching Penny, the intrepid junior girl detective in my favorite American cartoon, *Inspector Gadget*, which I only get to watch now while on vacations across the border.

One afternoon I walk home alone from school, arrive at my house, and realize I have no recollection of getting here. Nancy and Penny would never be so careless, I know. Pay more attention, I chide myself, as I search my mind for a memory of stepping through the leaves, or waiting at the corner for the crossing guard in the bright vest. What if someone tries to take you?

What is at risk?

Children are taken inexplicably; this is a proven fact. But other terrible things happen to them, too. One fall we all crowd around the television to see the emergency scene playing out in Midland, Texas, where a toddler named Jessica has fallen into an abandoned well. Baby Jessica is wedged in the well shaft twenty-two feet underground, and for fifty-eight hours the stations play every minute of her rescue effort, an unprecedented format for network news. When we leave for school, Baby Jessica is cooing and parched in the well but not dangerously dehydrated, her parents singing down to her; when we come back home in the afternoon the talking heads are giving her mere hours to live.

That night with the season's first snow a whisper in the sky, we eat dinner around the television. They must have even more KKK in Texas than they have in Florida, my mother muses, invoking one of the chilling reasons—men in white hats occasionally marching down our streets—that we eventually left the South to return to Canada. We watch the dust of the Lone Star State, a place we have never been and can't even imagine, swirl under media and construction lights inside our little TV box.

It's now or never, says the CBS News Special Report, and suddenly at 6:54 p.m. we understand that the long hours of waiting and tension and not knowing, which maybe have disturbed us more than we realize, are about to end.

People are moving in very close to the hole, the news announcer says. It looks like something is coming up.

We lean in toward the TV screen, stop chewing, hold our breath. And up she comes, battered but alive, a little girl strapped to a board, scraped and mud-caked. A miracle, people are saying. The crowd cheers, cameras snap and click, and soon, as our chicken wings grow cold, the search lights dim.

We would forget about that miracle and the nations of people who rooted for Jessica for two and a half days straight. But we would remember, us kids, how easy it is for someone you love to slip away.

The mother is the heart of the home

In our little suburb, our house address is 24, the same number, I learn at school, as the highest home in the land, 24 Sussex Drive, the White House of Canada. Where through much of my childhood Prime Minister Pierre Trudeau lives. Pierre's beautiful wife, Margaret, is much younger than her husband and unbeknownst to us is combatting the demons in her head even as she bears the leader of our great country three cherubic children. She has an affair and, when her youngest son is two, absconds, leaving Pierre (who later battles for and wins custody of the three kids) so she can study photography with Richard Avedon in New York and become a film star. This is scandal writ large. As I grow up, the name Margaret Trudeau slips off the tongues of adults, accompanied by a soft shake of the head. One time I hear the phrase She dropped her basket and I know what it means without knowing how I do.

What's really the problem here?

There's a certain kind of stare you get when your mother is an adulteress. It's an out-of-the-corner-of-the-eye stare, a wary look, a little pitying and more than a little angry. Adults in your hometown (and their daughters, to whom everything has been told or intimated) will give this look to you even when you're not standing next to your mother. Lately you get it more and more. Maybe it's because you look like her? Because now you're not ten, you're fourteen, you're fifteen, you have, more and more, the shape of a woman, the shape and maybe the face of women who dare to have sex with men other than their husbands.

You don't know why they are looking at you suspiciously.

Guilty by genetics and luck of the draw.

The truth can't be ignored forever

The year before you move to California you read *The Scarlet Letter* in English class. The book is a hot potato in your backpack, a shiny red apple on your night table. You begin to imagine there is a mini letter A (stitched in red fabric but also aflame) sewn onto you: the Daughter A, burning all the time, reappearing on every shirt no matter how often you change your outfit in search for a more flattering one.

Who is Jason?

We met the summer before I left for California. We were both sixteen, counselors-in-training at an overnight camp in the Laurentians. I first saw him when I came out of the shower house one morning, on the dirt trail to my bunk. My violet bra straps peeked out from my towel. Drumsticks poked out the back of his worn jeans pocket. For the first time a question etched itself onto my brain.

Saturday night camp dance. A startled pulling toward each other, like fireflies. Bottomless ideas / smoky campfire / legion of stars / lips worn raw with not-going-all-the-way-but-there's-so-much-else. Our tongues salted tributaries meeting, branching, meeting. And soon: the new sensation of speeding toward an objective I was not even aware existed only to arrive there as if at a cliff, precipitously, and achieve an absolute loss of control. Slip over the waterfall, a first spilling into myself that reclassified everything.

What is waiting for you?

1993

Right away I feel it as I step outside of the airport and inhale. Something is different here, something I can barely define but that I already know to the very core of my teenage body must be the essence of "Californian." The landscape is generous compared to back east: The streets are wide, this dry valley we seem to have landed in is wide, the trees are not so hefty or sentinel as to crowd us in or block anything out. Palm fronds wave languidly from two stories up and make a little *ffffwwppp* sound in the breeze. The air smells like sea salt and nectar and oranges, even here beside the inland freeway that rims the airport. There is nothing staid or weighty or static about this place, I conclude after only my first five minutes. It is giving, not taking. I close my eyes, and I feel it—her, the state—touch my skin with the cool palm of an open hand. I part my lips. I've been waiting for you, California whispers.

Hold it, not so fast—

"Crossing a border is not a simple thing. Getting anywhere ... now requires a constant producing of proof of identity. Who are you? You can't cross till we're sure," Ali Smith writes.

"Assimilation is a process of interpenetration and fusion in which persons and groups acquire the memories, sentiments, and attitudes of other persons or groups, and, by sharing their experiences and history, are incorporated with them in a common cultural life," write sociologists Robert E. Park and Ernest W. Burgess.

A cultural commons. Fusion.

Interpenetration.

What about *impenetration?*

Yes, yes. Surely the effort to assimilate must be necessarily marked by failures. As all impossible things are.

Unlikely things happening.

Unbearable things borne.

A place or a state of being can be impenetrable. When do I *really* cross over? It could happen any time: a drive alone through artichoke fields, spiky bulbs winking in the night; sex in the bed of an old Mazda pickup; the decline of a boy's letters in a mailbox; the question mark of a mountain; amidst fathers who come and go, who dissipate like fog; at the soft, charred bite of my first burrito; at the yielding.

Where will I belong? To whom?

This is what I want to know.

PART THREE

Interaction

Interaction

This is the main body of the interrogation, when the interrogator interacts with the respondent. This generally appears as a series of questions and responses.

All responses should be recorded for later analysis of body language.

This interaction may take place over a number of days and sessions, which may be limited or open ended in duration.

Rules[1] of the game

The rules cover both the interrogator (the *proponent*) and the person being interrogated (the *respondent*).

1. The respondent needs to take care not to inadvertently say something that might give out the information she wants to conceal or allow the proponent to infer it.

2. The proponent may coerce the respondent to reveal information through threats or sanctions, but only by the means allowed.

3. The proponent needs to pose questions to the respondent, and these questions can, and often should be, leading, loaded, and deceptive.

4. The respondent should answer in formulations that are vague, ambiguous, misleading, or confusing, if that will help serve her ends.

5. The proponent should probe critically into the respondent's prior replies and try to use them to extract information.

6. The respondent should take care to try to be consistent in her replies and in the commitments that can be inferred from them. Or she can wander.

7. If the proponent finds inconsistencies in the respondent's commitments, or implausible statements, or statements that are inconsistent with information from other sources, she should ask questions that critically examine them.

8. If the proponent extracts the information she wants from the respondent, then she has achieved her goal and the exercise concludes in her favor.

9. If the proponent terminates the interrogation without getting the information she wants, the exercise concludes in the respondent's favor. Unless the respondent had wanted to confess . . .

10. The two parties can use any arguments, even ones considered irrelevant or fallacious from the viewpoint of a critical discussion or outside audience, to achieve their ends.

---

1   This is a normative set of rules indicating what *should* happen, which is not necessarily what does happen in every case.

Where are you going?

After we landed in California, we made our way to our new house in a Bay Area suburb, half an hour from San Francisco. It came complete with top-of-the-line appliances, master soaking tub with skylight, bonus game room, palm-lined patio, and anti-allergen dusty rose pile rug. The house had a saccharine serviceableness in the form of Spanish / ranch / Mediterranean (an architecturally pasted-together mash, just like us).

I hoped it could absorb us the way we want to be absorbed.

I watched the movers carry in our things and set up my new room, the only bedroom downstairs and away from the others. So lucky, my mother whispered to me, glancing enviously at this separate space, far from the boys and her husband. I thought she was already out of love with Josef, or out of the idea of being in love. I didn't think he loved her either. But, I thought, probably lots of people in the world marry for convenience, salvage love for security's sake.

I gave her a hug. The walk-in closet and soaker tub would have to satisfy her.

You obviously knew where this was heading

Well.

The house itself probably gave us a clue.

Nothing that suburban, that pink and tiled and neatly subdi-vided, inside and out, could possibly contain anything real.

You know what happens when you want too much, don't you?

Frank Norris wrote the novel *McTeague* (1899), set in the San Francisco's Polk Gulch. It is considered an outstanding early example of American Naturalism, which used detailed realism to suggest that social conditions, heredity, and environment had an inescapable force in shaping human character. *McTeague* is the tale of a dentist from a poor miner's family who meets and marries Trina, the cousin of his best friend, Marcus. The couple wants the opportunity to build a certain type of life they aspire to: they have a vision. But from the start they are missing an essential ingredient, some alchemy needed for transmuting the baser metals of strategic companionship and social reaching into gold. Also, they just don't communicate very well. When the desire for opportunity and the struggle to survive life in the city overwhelms the couple and jealousy engulfs Marcus, they lose their moral way. Fate takes its course. The story might end in handcuffs in the most desperately un-overcomeable predicament you've ever read. What does this tell us?

There is no manner by which a person can control the destiny of their desires, whether or not they voice them.

Is it enough to just live?

No. You have to have your living go on record.

For example: The summer I was five my parents sent me to a day camp on the grounds of my school, adjacent to a large park with an elephant slide, a swing set, and a deep field of dry, honeydew-colored grass. My counselors were teenage girls with teeny shorts and their eyes on the boy counselors. They ignored us. They smacked their gum. On days when it poured a summer rain they crowded us into the chalet and made us watch *Rocky* on VHS, visions of dripping boxer blood mixing with rivulets of mud on the filthy chalet floor. One day I roamed the field farther and farther until I got lost, stumbling finally through the butter-scented heat into the shade of a weeping willow tree, where I put my head between my scabby knees and waited behind the braided green curtain to be found.

Another time we fingerpainted large posters outside. My best friend, Randi, and I, our little palms inked indigo, were sent into the cool, deserted school building to wash our hands. On the way in, I spotted the round concrete pillars in the school's entryway. Smooth and cylindrical. A deserted school. Two unsupervised five-year-olds. Of course I pressed my pudgy hand onto that pillar, spreading the purple paint, defacing, demarcating. The painted print of my hand sponged where it shouldn't be was my own oration, a claiming.

I was questioned by the counselors, given the opportunity to speak. Did you put paint prints on the school? It's fine, just tell us the truth.

At the moment of the asking I had to make a choice. To give a person who questions you the answer they want to hear is to cede your power, to hand over dominion of your own experience. Even five-year-olds know this. I silently shook my head no.

What did your friends and family say to you, a girl of sixteen, when you moved away?

Once in a lifetime opportunity!
Make the best of it.
So many doors will open.
Aren't you afraid of the gangs?
You must be excited.
Ah, to be young again.
Whole life ahead of you.
Hit the immigration jackpot, eh?
We all have to make choices now don't we?
Headed to the Promised Land.
U. S. of A.!
Going stateside?

State your side

Why do I have to take sides?

What exactly were you (and your mother) running from?

"Seventy-three percent of those who identified [California] in this way used adventure and opportunity as code words for 'escape from community.' In the towns and rural neighborhoods ... in which they lived, community was created through cooperation and judgment. In essence, both were used to measure who was a part of the group and who was not," writes California historian Denise S. Spooner. "Some migrants found this aspects of community repressive."

Did you want to go, or not?

In the months leading up to our move, while my mother and step-father consulted real estate agents, lawyers, immigration agencies, and school districts, I prepared for California from the bathroom. My method of indoctrination was simple. After dinner, when the various factions of our step-family would retreat to their bunkers, I locked myself in the downstairs bathroom and spread out my cache: fashion magazines; brochures for American universities with glossy pictures of grinning, soft-haired freshman lounging on fresh green quads; a real-estate guide picturing Spanish-tiled homes with blazing pink bougainvillea and the sparkling, kidney-shaped swimming pools of perpetual summer. And, of course, my journal, where I listed all the things that could be great about California and all the accouterments (new clothes, a carefully engineered popularity increase achieved by starting fresh in a place where no one knew me) that would help me assimilate quickly.

To assimilate in California would mean to live. To not assimilate, I knew before I even left the invisible walls of my home town, would be to fail to live.

Would that mean to die?

It might have. Some things I don't remember.

It sounds like you want to have your cake and eat it too

The author long having had an anxious desire to visit those wild regions upon the great Pacific, which had now become the topic of conversation in every circle, and in reference to which speculations both rational and irrational were everywhere in vogue, now determined to accomplish her desired object.

So your testimony is one of willingness?

There are always things left behind, and new tactics we need to accommodate them (tactics may be readied). Left behind: people; badges of shame; yellow tickets; friends; fathers, minefields of fathers.

Certainties are left behind.

And perfect boys in ratty jeans who read Dostoyevsky and climb on top of you and make you come.

Are we detecting a backdrop of sadness?

Our new step-father, Josef, was a brilliant engineer. If we were to believe his stories, which we did, he was also a former elite Israeli soldier in the Six-Day War. He was stiff, analytical, awkward with emotion. Corny and good-natured until you got on his bad side.

Most importantly, Josef's first wife and youngest son, their third child, were run over by a taxi as they crossed a street while on vacation in New York City a few years before he met my mother. Horrified, just out of the frame of the picture of ultimate devastation, Josef, Asher, and Ric had watched the crash from the sidewalk. This is something you don't ever travel back from.

Leverage emotional relationships

They met on a blind date when my mother was thirty-seven. I was gone at sleepaway camp, so Suzanne, my best friend, babysat my little brothers during the date. As soon as I got back from camp a couple weeks later, before my duffel bag was even emptied of its stinky socks and long underwear, Suzanne cornered me.

Holy fuck no! she said. Her dark eyes narrowed, her straight black bangs gleaming like a fourteen-year-old version of Uma Thurman from *Pulp Fiction*. He showed up at the door with a fruitcake! First date and he brings your mother a fucking fruitcake! It can't happen. Sorry. Like. No.

Just over a year later, the night before their wedding, they had a huge fight. Maybe he felt the threat of my mother's outwardly projected sexiness, her less-than-100-percent affection for him. Maybe she knew that trading financial uncertainty, single parenting, and tater tot dinners for what he brought to the table would silence a part of her soul. Ghosts roamed among us. Even before we became a family we all wondered whether there would be enough elastic to actually hold us together. For how long could it stretch.

That night they screamed. It was an interrogation, him of her. Do you still love him? You had better never say that sonofabitch's name again in this house.

My mother's loyalty (her body?) was on trial.

Doors slammed. I "ran away" up the street in the dark for a few hours—to protest, I guess. Later, my mother sat with me on my bed, her brown eyes red, while the rest of the household, exhausted, folded back into quiet. It's going to be fine, do you hear me? I'm going to make this work. I promise, she said, reaching to embrace me. We'll be okay. Don't you believe in me?

Yes. I believed her. More than anyone. There was a reason for all of this, there had to be. Something that, in the end, would make it all worthwhile. We were still in Montreal then; California was not yet on my step-father's radar. But under my sheets that night before their wedding, I confessed to myself my yearning for a drastic change in my own topography, a pull outward, like ocean waves.

Can we agree on a final version here?

I wanted to be reconstituted.

What did your family do for fun?

We went on outings to better soak in our surroundings, like you do the mineral-scented hot pools of a Marin County spa, and also to better immerse ourselves in one another.

There is a lot to see, Josef told us, wielding the new minivan into mint-scented redwood forests and guiding the awed clump of us beneath the skylight enclosures of soaring, movie-set malls.

We had been in the States for a month. My mother and stepfather had been married just over a year. It was still summer but edging close to fall, which I learned made no difference in the suburbs of East Bay. While San Francisco was often shrouded in cool, misty fog, rising before us like a mythological kingdom as we emerged from the cabled shadows of the Bay Bridge, it was still hot and dry out here, just fifteen miles east of the Pacific. The mounds and knolls rippled away from the city's earthquaked hills like gentle aftershocks, yellow and bare. The sky was a naked blue, broken only by the loop of a hawk hunting over the white and peach subdivisions.

The furnace of late August was making us grouchy; we were used to intense bouts of East Coast sweat rewarded by blasts of air conditioning, but not this. Each time we piled into the van we bickered over how high to turn up the air, how soon it felt cool enough to breathe again. That bickering led to other bickering: which Californian food to eat for lunch (In-N-Out burgers, the ubiquitous soup-and-salad bars where you could get almost anything you wanted together on one plate, the new-to-us world of burritos); when to stop for a bathroom break; which direction to the national historic monument; who lost the colorful state map complete with glossy pictorials of California's state animal (grizzly bear), state flower (golden poppy), and state bird (valley quail).

One morning while the five of us kids and our parents drove north toward Gold-Rush-era Sacramento, a new song I liked, Salt-N-Pepa's "Shoop," came on the radio.

Turn this up, I called to my mother, who obediently adjusted the dial.

Asher did not like pop music.

Change the station, he grumbled from the minivan's third row as we barreled down the highway and I launched my off-pitch sing-along, grinding my ass in my seat to what I recognized even then as a feminist sex anthem.

No, don't change it, this is good! I shouted.

I knew it was a tease even as I belted it, the coded lyrics giving way to the line about licking the hot guy like a lollipop should be licked.

SHUT IT OFF, roared Asher, his insta-rage like the suddenly flicked-on siren of an ambulance. And before anyone in the car knew what hit us, he unclicked his seatbelt, torpedoed from the far back of the van through the middle seats all the way to the front console, and slammed his fist into the off button of the radio tuner.

As we barreled down the highway, all was quiet on our western front.

How do we know this is true?

Geography is a never-ending dialogue between the real and the imagined. For approximately two hundred years, between the sixteenth century and the year 1747, when King Ferdinand VI of Spain issued a decree to the contrary, Europeans believed California was an island, cut off from the mainland by a liminal oceanic channel and depicted on hand-drawn maps as a kind of mystical floating member ("the large and goodly island of California" one 1625 map by Englishman Henry Briggs labeled it).

According to a study of the myth by essayist Rebecca Solnit, who uncovers the following information with the help of G. Salim Mohammed, a digital and rare maps librarian at Stanford, the first mention of the island of California comes in 1510 from Garci Rodriguez de Montalvo's *Las Sergas de Esplandián*. Maps, like many artistic creations, are referential, so this first mention, fully imagined by Montalvo, became *de rigueur* on maps that followed. Even when Father Eusebio Kino's travels from 1698 to 1701 confirmed the firm attachment of California to the mainland and documented that attachment on a map entitled "A Passage by Land to California," it took another half century for the island to find itself reattached in other North American atlases.

Dreams have a way of inking themselves onto history the way a cartographer's colors seep brightly into parchment.

Do you solemnly swear you did not have improper thoughts about your step-brother Asher?

In my bed in California I tried to learn how to masturbate. I wanted to return to the feeling of slipping over the waterfall, of the world spun into oblivion. But I could not get it right. At sixteen I did not know how to navigate myself, how to circle something in a way that does not return you to the same beginning. Quietly I groped at the threshold between one thing and something else, trying to map my territory, trying to fall off the edge of the world.

What can you reveal about that time?

We covered much ground that first month: a tortuously hot family hike up Mt. Tamalpais; the hellishly hotter Six Flags amusement park in the flat, fast-food-littered North Bay, where the blacktop of infinite parking lots smelled like burned rubber and threatened to reach up and choke us before we made it to the front ticket booth; the San Francisco Aquarium; the breezy Monterey boardwalk, where the clam chowder was so sweet and rich that I wanted to slide into a bowl of it and drink until I drowned.

We hit malls, trekked trails, rode clanging trolleys, and as we went we shed things. The heavier clothes we'd brought from the northern climate of our home country were folded and stuffed into the pink house's many closets (but not donated or thrown away, because the threads that tied us to whence we came were not something any of us were ready to cut just yet—on this we all silently agreed).

As we shed the heavier things, slowly, we bought new, light-weight items. Hair was cut and highlighted. My mother and I, following the lead of the smiling, sunny women and teenage girls we saw everywhere, traded in our plain fingernails for the long, glossy acrylics tipped with glowing white French manicures that are part of the California female dress code.

We collected small souvenirs on our outings, tokens to remind us where we'd been. At each stop we browsed the trinket stores for seashells that may have come up out of the surf or from a Chinese factory that pressed them into believably smooth, pink, and speckled orbs; shot glasses; postcards; hound-stooth candy in small drawstring bags; gold panning sets; Mystery Spot magnets; crystal-filled geodes you could crack open with a sharp blow, like the heart.

In one of these interchangeable stores I picked out a California license plate key chain imprinted with my name, conveniently seven letters long, across the palm-tree-bordered plate. Though I'd turned sixteen back in the spring, I wasn't driving yet. The license plate key chain reminded me that I would be soon and that whatever car I would end up driving would actually have the word California scrawled on its plate. I hung the key chain on the bulletin board in my bedroom, crowded already with the ephemera of my existence thus far—concert tickets, invites to the parties of my Canadian friends, love letters from Jason—tangible evidence that I was collecting a life.

While we toured, Josef was imprinting the social and geographical structures of California onto his memory, analyzing maps and downloading the facts and history of our new surroundings like an undercover special-forces agent who must store all his information in his mind.

There are missions every eighty miles, universities every forty, he lectured. Just look at these freeway on-ramps! The sound walls are capable of blocking out…

My mother, meanwhile, operated on cruise control, admiring the shops and views. Like a sound wall, she blocked out Josef and the family disharmony.

On one of our last tourist trips, just before Labor Day, we wandered the quaint streets of Petaluma, the poppy-colored Golden Gate Bridge arching into the mist behind us. There is a picture of us, taken by a well-meaning fellow tourist. We are sitting in a row on a brick wall: Josef's long, ropy arm is thrown over Asher's sagging shoulder; my mother sits almost a full body-width away from Josef, squeezed up against my smiling little brother Zachary, his golden hair haloed like an angel in the never-ending sun. The two middle boys ignore the camera and punch each other off the edge of the wall. I am at the end of the line, one leg crossed over the other knee, hair in a ponytail and new sunglasses shielding my eyes, looking down, examining my new pedicure.

Later I will try to recall the names of all the places I went in California, the spaces I passed through and passed through me, their location, their feel, like a gouge in the granite of some northern mountain. But I remember few details, so much feeling and so few facts. Gouge, the word, is so close to gauge, as in measure, as in witness, as in all the minutes and hours and days spent silently gauging my own level of comfort, or discomfort. My belonging. Gauging the likelihood of my voice catching in my throat.

What is the relationship between confession and extinction?

This is the second instance of interrogation, the second memory.

Before we could settle into the new house and our new schools we had to make a family pilgrimage to San Francisco to the United States Naturalization and Immigration Office for our interview. We had arrived in the USA on special lottery visas, which would, if we were well-behaved and productive immigrants, eventually lead to green cards and permission to stay forever.

But first we had to prove that we were who we claimed to be. In our family this could be harder than it sounded.

As our new seven-seater minivan glided west over the East Bay freeways, passing other clean-shaven suburbs, Josef counseled us: They are going to want to know that we are a real family, that we are not just together to get green cards, okay? So they might ask you questions about our habits. Try to answer well.

We all nodded. Maybe, I thought to myself, the immigration agents would ask me about the wedding, about the night before, how our families joined. About what came before that.

This filled me with dread.

When we arrived across the swooping steel of the Bay Bridge, the immigration office, inside the belly of a San Francisco tower, teemed with people from every corner of the world. We crowded into rows of plastic seats, thighs and shoulders pressing, babies squealing and languages flying, inhaling each other's lunch meat, hair products, breast milk.

Finally, we were called to be separately interviewed. I went into a room with a broad-shouldered female agent who closed the door and motioned for me to sit in a chair across a small desk from the chair she sat in.

Why did you come to California? she asked.

State your purpose. Confess your longing or be expelled.

I thought about Jason on top of me, moving in a slowly circular motion. I thought about Dara C. in my Canadian high school, with the perfect red hair and the popular friends and the cold blue eyes that stared right through me, evidence of my invisibility. I thought about my mother and father and me, on the Florida beach, digging and lounging, a lost world before everything else.

What does your step-father do for work?

On the table was a manila folder, many of the details of my sixteen years of life no doubt inside. What did they know about my mother and father? About me, us? Suddenly this interview seemed to be a minefield.

I sensed that my future hinged on these slow-motion minutes inside a windowless room with a uniformed American immigration officer. I had entered on a plane a couple of months ago, but this was my plea for passage.

I could throw this whole interview on purpose right now by telling the truth, I thought, and maybe—likely—we'd all be riding another jet back home to Canada before my pale skin even took on a tan. My mother didn't marry Josef for a green card, but we certainly were not a family with the promise of succeeding.

Instead, I tried my best to be lovingly convincing.

What is your step-father's favorite food? The officer asked, leaning in, her hands clasped on the metal table.

Tabbouleh, I answered, thinking of the lemony grit of the Israeli cilantro-bulgur salad.

What do you do for fun as a family?

Watch movies. Go shopping. Go to movies. We, um, we go on outings.

I smiled like a good girl who adored her family. It was true, we occasionally went to the grocery store all together, if only to make sure everyone got food they were willing to eat, because none of us liked the same things.

The questions remain strangely random: How is your parents'

bedroom decorated? What do they like to do together? What music does your step-brother like best?

When did your mother and step-father get married?

Last winter. I made a gesture with my hands toward my heart, indicating how precious the wedding memories were to me.

What was the wedding like?

It was pretty small, just in the synagogue. We dressed up. Our grandparents were there, they were so *overjoyed*, I raved, the answers rough on my tongue. We ate tabbouleh.

I must have passed, I understood, because soon I was delivered back to my family, where we signed papers with our lawyer, who described to us the laws we must obey and warned us to never, ever get involved with drugs, the one thing America might not tolerate from people like us.

We emerged with our matching manila folders from the concrete and steel of the high-rise onto honking, color-smeared Market Street in downtown San Francisco. The thick palms waved at us and the sun was a big, warmth-giving ball moving toward the flat west of the Sunset District and the Pacific Ocean beyond.

It felt like we survived an elimination round in an epic challenge, a near-death experience in a blockbuster action movie. Like we won something. Warriors, we had proved that we were not scammers, that we knew and loved each other well and were not the product of a fraudulently crafted green-card marriage.

Funny, though, I thought to myself as I inhaled the salty sea air as far into my lungs as it would come, that we barely knew each other. Compared to the lure and potential of a new American life, each side of our family seemed expendable to the other.

I was starting to suspect, squinting into the giant orange sun, that we were all just degrees of throwaway.

What proof do you have?

The above application for change of nonimmigrant status is approved. The new status, and length of authorized temporary stay in this status, for the named applicant(s) is indicated above.

The nonimmigrant status of the applicant(s) is based on the separate nonimmigrant status held by a principal alien based on authorized employment in the United States.

Make a copy of this notice for each applicant. She must keep the copy with her Form I-94, Nonimmigrant Arrival-Departure Document and must present it when requested by INS. However, the copy does not need to be turned into INS when she leaves the U. S.

However, each applicant must turn in her Form I-94 when leaving the U. S.

What is a suburban American high school?

It is white and spiraling outward from itself like a nautilus, appearing to unfurl but in fact always tightly knotted, tethered to what it knows.

It is white.

It is the laboratory of American assimilation.

It is bouncy cheerleaders and rock-hard jocks. It is everyone else moving out of their way.

It is an inborn American spirit nurtured since babyhood. It is something unknowable called a pep rally. It is terror in the halls. It is hiding in the library. It is bulimia in the girls' bathrooms, which makes you vow, Never.

It is walking fast, staring straight ahead to look very busy as though you cannot be interrupted at any cost.

It is blond to your brunette, ripe for picking to your still-clinging-scared-to-the-vine.

It is a parking lot of shiny big trucks jacked into the air on wheels as large as the egos and wished-for dicks of the boys who drive them.

It is alien, but much less so than you.

Did you have any friends?

As the weeks progressed I kept to myself and made no real Californian friends. Every night, I cradled my phone receiver to my ear while 3,000 miles away my best friend in Montreal, Suzanne, did the same.

No! Are they fucking for real? she asked about the lustrous cheerleaders I described and the kids who came to school from out in Danville and beyond, the far eastern, still semi-rural reaches of the Bay Area, with cowboy hats and horseshit-caked leather boots. And then she'd tell me about what all my old friends were doing and update me on life in her house, where she lived miserably with her docile mother and drunk grandfather. She kept a running tally of the next time we would see each other—106 days, 94 days, 68 days. On days that had been hard for either one of us we lay in our beds and drifted off to sleep with our phones, the sound of the other's breathing over the line.

What else did you learn in the American school?

The Donner Party is the wagon train of eighty-seven American pioneers who, inspired by the philosophy of Manifest Destiny, found themselves trapped by snow late in the fall of 1846 while trying to cross the Sierra Nevadas on their journey to California. Part of the problem was the party tried to save time by taking a new route, a shortcut called Hastings Cutoff, which they were led to believe would be an easy crossing but in fact delayed them dangerously. Thirty-nine members of the party died from starvation, exposure, disease, and trauma. Famously, some of the survivors resorted to cannibalism, turning a relatively unimportant pioneer party into one of the most spectacular tragedies in California history and the story of western migration.

Western migration. Those words rolled off my newly Californian tongue with a sense of sanction. A historical endorsement that placed me into a diorama of comings-and-goings. I was with pioneers. I was with buffalo. I was with computer-minded Indian families in saris, and geese coming south before the snows. Swept along in a great wave, I could fade into the background until I found footing. Despite the gruesome details, the Donner story comforted me. There were others before me, a caravan of them, who left their pasts and overcame their presents in a quest for the thing called home. Reinvention was possible. You just had to be willing to consume anything.

List the things in the American mall

Hot Topic, where you can buy knee-high black lace-up boots, black lipstick, Wicked Witch of the West striped tights, and dresses that look like Morticia Addams nighties. You dabble only, effecting a fumbling mix of suburban prep with a dash of the gothic.

The Gap. They did not have this store, along with so many other American touchstones, in the Canada you came from. Inside, the rows of baggy jeans and brand-emblazoned hoodies make you swoon. You find a mustard-colored, knee-length cable knit sweater and are only slightly surprised to realize you suddenly believe that owning it would change your life.

The food court. This is not the shopworn food court of the Cavendish Mall, that dismal neighborhood mall of your youth, where Yoda-like bubbies ambled about collecting gefilte fish and halvah in plastic bags and the popular girls from the private Jewish day school up the road from your disintegrating public high school gathered around chiseled-jaw boys in letter jackets and nibbled hand-cut steak fries out of paper cups. No. This is every global food group under the sun, co-opted into simple softness and Americanized meal deals, available beneath soaring mall skylights. The only difficulty is making the choice.

American mall smell. You smelled it a few times on trips, and when you lived in the South when you were small. But now you can sniff any time you like, and you do: You inhale that scent as deeply as you can, Eau de Possibility. Odor of freshly uncrated product. Of unlimited new identities. You want to ask the woman at the Macy's perfume counter (but you don't), Do you have this, maybe in a cologne? This smell of American Mall?

Victoria's Secret. Her secret, it turns out, is that she knows how to transform average American breasts into glitter-dusted pillows of silken-cupped femininity, and that this transformation is compulsory. You quickly obtain a selection of underthings in breathy colors, studded with tiny faux crystals so your body, when the time (surely, soon) comes, can be pleasing to your viewing public.

At the mall frequently, my mother and I were disciples. The East Bay housewives and their teenage daughters were our unwitting deities.

Do we need this? my mother would ask casually but a little loudly, holding aloft a breezy Donna Karan wrap dress on a Wednesday morning when I should have been sitting in statistics class. My mother came alive in the American mall, shining and happy and optimistic as if on display. Here we could keep each other company, comfortably, and work hard on what mattered most: acculturating.

Yes, I would confirm, scouring the MAC counter for a new color I had seen Erin, a popular cheerleader in my homeroom, wearing. A few swipes of Josef's American Express Premier card and we'd head to the California Pizza Kitchen, settle in on the patio by a burbling simulated river, order Thai crunch salads, and carefully study the schools of bleached hair and shopping bags floating by.

Where do you think you're going?

The road ribbons out. Endless lanes forward, back, adjacent, a concrete football field undulating in every direction. I have a car. Someone has handed me the keys. At first I cannot make it move smoothly. I haven't learned stick shift, but to spread out stipulates stick shifting, so I get up to speed; soon I move beyond jerk and stall to a place of mastery.

I coast, over under over. Pass palms, houses, hills, buildings of each decade, sun on factory walls. Pink, jade, softest mauves.

I am beginning to love her, California. Every direction is a new part of her mapped body, wild grasses like silky hair. Kidney swimming pools; flower-bud breath; warm-arteried highways. From my driver's seat I look out at her, speeding by, left behind, always reappearing up ahead, with the wish for reflection: were these windows mirrors they might show a navigable self back to me, bright and busy, traveling toward purpose.

State of awe: I am touching this curve of beautiful earth.

A dream I've had takes many forms. Sometimes I am plowing along an elevated speedway, in a place that feels like a version of Berkeley or Stanford but Seussian. And right at the outermost arc my car flies off the road, soars through the air quietly, and calmly in my subconscious I anticipate the head-heart-stomach drop that is about to jettison me from this life. The way you prepare for a massive dip on the roller coaster. Not a yielding but a bracing.

Someone has handed me the keys. The roads stretch out ahead. The highway of California snakes everywhere: spellbinding essssssses. Now all I need to do is navigate, stick to the curves, shift the stick, lean into the bend of the smooth S shapes. Press. Swell. Release. Slope. Adhere to the shifts. Stay the course.

We have the letters your boyfriend Jason wrote to you

September 2

Too many things to say on paper, so listen to the tape again. I got your letter. So you liked the mountains from the plane? I'm happy to hear you arrived at your destination safely. I've looked hard to find it on a map, but I haven't. I will continue to look at our picture. To think about that thunderstorm.

September 19

Somehow I knew I would hear from you today. Sucks the other letter was returned. Tim the football player with the I.Q. less than his shoe size probably has a relative working at the post office who could not find Canada on a map. You are my last thought when I go to sleep. Hope you like the picture of Hendrix.

January 22

Because when I look into your eyes our love shines like a diamond mine.

February 2

We're so perfect together.

I'm nearing my sexual peak in a year.

I don't believe it will be possible to co-exist without each other.

February 5

Today I found a piece of writing. It is gospel in a sense:

You might say I'm catagoraphobic. I hate getting stuffed into pigeonholes. I run the other way when people try to tell me who I am. So don't try to figure me out. Just enjoy me. Or maybe I should say just enjoy us. There are so many different facets to my personality that monogamy with me will feel like a promiscuous feast to you. I can teach you secrets you didn't even know existed. I can take you on a tour of the ultimate taboos without your even guessing we've sailed off the edge of the known world.

February 17

I am going crazy over you.

February 27

I dream of you. Months of frustration and longing.

What aren't you telling us?

I dreamed of Jason. I imagined that after that first year in California, after the state transformed me into whatever she would, made me better—cleansed me—I would go back to Montreal. I would attend college there, a different person, Californian now. In my dream Jason waited for me, turning out his prolific letters on white school looseleaf, ready to receive me back just in time for his sexual peak.

I dreamed of us lying in a field beneath starred ribbons of galaxy.

I dreamed of the way he was in love with books and the way he whispered words into my mouth.

I dreamed of him exploring even the insides of me, of filling a need California had so far been unable to satisfy.

I dreamed of a centrifugal force.

Go back into the unknown

Once in the year I was ten I saw a canary standing outside our front door in the snow. It was Montreal's November, the first storm of the season, and the white mounds had piled up overnight on the street, the stoop, the boughs of every tree, sparkly and unsullied. I spied the patch of yellow through the window in our vestibule and yelled for my mother to come. She opened the heavy black door with the *Twenty-Four* scrawled in cursive above, scooped up the bird in surprise and slammed the door.

Can we keep it, can we? I asked, reaching on tip-toe to see the thing, which seemed to shiver down to its miniature bones. How had it survived? Where had it come from?

She frowned, shook her feathered hair, and went to the kitchen for a warm towel.

My mother was busy, with laundry and diaper changes and scrubbing the upstairs bathroom, where white mold mushrooms grew from the caulking of the mint green tub no matter how often she tore them away and scorched it with bleach. In between batches of broiled hamburgers and vacuuming, she loved us. Yet at the edges of my girl mind I could not completely ignore the bouts of personality shift—snapping or swatting at us kids, sinking utterly into her afternoon episode of *Days of Our Lives* where the women were always fancily made-up and embroiled in passionate melees, even the housewives—an ennui I can only now begin to understand.

Can we please, please, please keep it? I begged, gazing at the canary, improbable yet here, confined in an upside-down colander our square wood table.

I'll talk to your father when he gets home, she said. Which wasn't good. We were dog people. A bird, I knew, was not in the family handbook.

By morning, the bird was gone. I wasn't sure where but I hoped to a generous bird-loving granny in the neighborhood or, at least, a pet store. Why did the bird come if I couldn't keep it? Things felt like they should go one way but instead always seemed to go another. Maybe that is being ten, I thought.

What is it like in the wilderness?

Soon after the canary arrived it was Hanukkah, and my grandparents bought me a book called *Into the Unknown*, a guide to UFOs, aliens, clairvoyance, telepathy, animal ESP, mind-over-matter, reincarnation, ghosts and poltergeists, earth shrines, Atlantis, witchcraft, and more. I read the book daily, wearing the pages soft, committing the facts and rumors to memory.

Do you want to hear about the Bermuda Triangle or Stonehenge? I asked my mother one afternoon over the school's holiday break. She was folding laundry in the winter sunlight streaming through the window.

Why do you want to know about all of that? she asked, holding up my father's white underwear. She looked at me, the wrinkle on her forehead like a fissure in time.

It's cool, I ventured. They're like these mysteries and everybody is trying to figure out the answers.

I thought I could make her see what was so important about these unexplained phenomena, that I could sell her on the value of probing the unknown, of poking until we could maybe uncover what lay concealed.

But she had already turned away.

We know you know what a whore is

I know that the year I was ten my mind was heightened to the signs of romance. When the movie *Dirty Dancing* came out, with its posters of Jennifer Grey in metallic shoes mamboing in the muscled arms of Patrick Swayze, I pleaded with my mother to take me. I have to go! I begged, waving my own pink ballet shoes in her face. I'm a dancer! I did feel the movie would improve my jazz steps, but there was another, unnamable pull, too, the little lurch my lower stomach made when I thought about a man and woman dancing closely, when I thought about Darell/Daryl at school with their mix of rough boyishness and still-downy cheeks ruddy from the playground.

She agreed to take me. But she went first with her friend Lisa, and that night when she came home from the theater she shook her head at me definitively—I was not old enough to see *Dirty Dancing*. Sorry, but it's final. Her hips seemed loose as she glided to her bedroom.

As the heavy northern winter settled in that year, my Barbies began doing strange things with each other down in our basement rec room. Sometimes one of the girls and Ken would go out to a ball and then afterward they'd drive home in Malibu Barbie's pink convertible, Ken would come inside, they would have a snack in the Dream Kitchen and then Barbie and Ken would lie down in her glow-in the-dark canopy bed with Ken on top. I wasn't sure what they were doing or why, but If I heard anyone's footsteps coming downstairs I would quickly rearrange Barbie and Ken back in the car or in the Dream Pool outside, my mouth pressed into silence, my heart pounding in my slight chest.

We are going to need you to stop looking away

I spent a lot of time with my brothers. Steven five years younger than me, Zachary ten years younger, almost like a little son of my own. On dark autumn afternoons while the wind stripped the maple trees outside, I played the Disney movies on a loop and rocked the baby in my lap. His pale, soap-scented hair curled softly beneath my chin. While Cinderella sang to her mice and Alice fell down, down, down, I buttered toast and poured milk. I read book after book, sounding out stories slowly, eventually teaching them both to read, to be open to the wonder of words formed of letters that could be assembled to mean anything, anything in the world.

"I'll love you forever, I'll like you for always," I read from the beloved words of Robert Munsch. "As long as I'm living, my baby you'll be."

So you caught them red-handed?

The year I turned eleven the spring sun glinted brightly off the melting snowdrifts outside when I plodded into the kitchen early one afternoon.

What, my mother exclaimed. She seemed surprised to see me. My father was at work.

Had I come upstairs unexpectedly from playing with my Barbies in the basement? Was I home sick that day from the fifth grade with the flu? Something was out of sorts for me to be home in pajamas in the middle of a weekday. I wore my frilly Smurfette nightgown and bare feet. Upstairs, my new baby brother slept softly in the old yellow crib.

My mother's apple cake was in the oven, its blossomy smell filling the house. And there was a strange man in our kitchen, leaning at an angle against the butcher-block topped dishwasher, his shaggy blond hair swooped casually to the side. My mother took a small step away from him as I entered. Her red nails disappeared behind her back, a smile at the corner of her lips.

I ignored a ripple in my stomach.

Go back and play, my mother said quickly, and I'll bring you some cake.

I turned away from them, unable to shake the feeling that the man looked too comfortable in our kitchen with its funny white-and-maroon checked wallpaper and chocolate brown appliances, too at ease in the space where we sat every night, my parents, brothers and I, eating Shake 'n Bake chicken and Shepherd's pie.

As I left the kitchen I heard my mother whisper, The baby will be up soon—then I'll bring him down.

Why would a strange blond man want to see our baby? I wondered.

What does it mean to be good?

Be a good girl, my grandmother would urge me. What a good girl, they would say when I kept my hands in my lap and sat still at the symphony and ballet or stepped lightly at the art museum. Such a good girl, my mother and the women around me would praise when I had slipped quietly into the background, was helpful when asked, when I flashed a good report card, or tossed out a wry quip to a group of adults. That favorite small triumph I liked best of all because it was adults' attention I wanted most. Good was silent, except when, able to impress or delight, it wasn't. What's the matter with you? My mother would ask, annoyed, when I prodded, poked, challenged, asked too many questions or inserted myself too much. Shut your mouth, she'd say to me. Watch yourself.

What are the conditions under which confession is possible?

The third interrogation:

It was not a dream. At least not to begin with. I did go to court.

In the spring of our first year in California, my youngest brother Zachary's father sued my mother for full custody so he could bring Zachary, seven, back to Montreal.

A new outfit was purchased for me: short black skirt with narrow pleats, form-fitting multicolored sweater, low patent leather heels, the nicest clothes I owned.

I understood my role without anyone spelling it out for me. My family wanted me to testify, to tell the truth—that my mother was a *good* mother and that we, my brothers and I and our mother, needed to stay together as a family. That being torn apart would be bad. My role was to fix this situation, to tell the truth, the truer truth that would overpower the other truth, that my mother had cheated on her husband and ended up pregnant and had a child and loved that child and the man who fathered him even though he later turned away from her. My role was to speak for us all, to save us. I took it on willingly. I knew I could correct everything.

But is this version of events believable?

I can testify to what I remember happening. I flew to Montreal with my mother. I dressed in the fancy outfit. My grandparents and mother and aunt and uncle and lawyers spoke in hushed voices in a room off the courthouse hallway. Then I was led into the courtroom, to a polished wooden witness box in the corner.

I had to open the low door in the box, step up to the inside, then close it behind me. My junior miss heels went *click click click.*

State your name for the record, said the judge from his bench.

When your voice disappears, I would later learn, there is always an instigating sorrow. A censure you quickly adopt as your own.

In the box my heart began to throb, my skin to burn. I ached to become invisible. A fear I had not prepared for—they had not prepared me for—that I could now not get away from.

Silence is a disappearance.

STATE YOUR NAME FOR THE RECORD HE SAID.

Disappearance is an erasure.

STATE ███████████HE R████████ SA█D.

In the end, I could not speak.

Is form a response to silence?

I have read about form as a response to doubt, which leads me to ask whether I should interrogate the way this testimony is set up (this testimony).

Doubt > 1175-1225; (v.) Middle English *douten* < Anglo-French, Old French *douter* < Latin *dubitāre* to waver, hesitate, be uncertain (frequentative of OL *dubāre*), equivalent to dub- doubt + -it- frequentative suffix + āre infinitive suffix; (noun) Middle English *doute* < Anglo-French, Old French, derivative of the v.

Doubt > Disbelieve > Not believable > Unbelievable > Disbelieving > Disbelief > State of Disbelief > State.

In literature an unsympathetic character is one who is not believable. Even if she is realistic, your character might not be believed, or liked, by your readers. Like when you are on the stand and you are asked to state your name to save your family and you say ... nothing.

Try a tactic of resistance

If you don't want the interrogator to know anything you know, say the following:

I am invoking my right to silence and decline further comment without the presence of legal counsel.

In the vast majority of cases, interview over, period.

Or? If you want the interrogator to know what you want them to know, simply say the following:

I am invoking my right to speech and decline further silence in the presence of legal counsel.

If you fail at this: In the vast majority of cases, interview over, period.

What else do you know?

I can tell you what I know happened but do not remember because later others told me it did.

Before the courtroom, an attorney for the other side (Witness deposition? Checking for *bad*? A clumsy probe into the epigenetics of 'slut'?) asked me, in preparation for my testimony about my family life, about the love and affection my siblings and I had for each other, about the importance of a safe and unbroken home: Are you sexually active?

Are you sexually active, he asked me in the moments just before I took the witness stand in open court.

I was sixteen.

Outline for us your sexual history

My first real kiss was with David R. He was in my social circle but more popular than me. His grandmother lived on the same street as mine did, and every Friday night for Shabbos both of us would sit inside those steamy, onion-scented houses with our families while the white moon rose over the Jewish suburbs of Montreal and all the other people doing the same rehearsed customs.

One fall night after dinner, I walked to David's grandmother's house and rang the doorbell. I do not know what gave me the courage to do this. At fourteen, though, a timer in me had been turned on, an urge was ticking toward fulfillment.

We went for a walk to the baseball field, talking about things I don't remember. A sense of predetermination followed us; we both knew without saying it what was intended. At home plate we stopped and turned toward each other. My bobbed hair, straightened mercilessly and shiny in the cold night air, grazed my check. He leaned in and our lips touched, then our tongues. I know I was wearing a silky ivory shirt, and his large boy's hand slipped up the side of it, rotating expertly to cup my left breast.

Later I giggled on the phone with my friend Carole and thought about the warmth from his hand over the silk of my shirt. What did it mean that we had kissed like that? Would we date? Would he tell people I was his girlfriend?

But later that month, while I was returning my clarinet in its black box to the shelf after band, David slipped into the small instrument room and thrust his mouth on mine, his hand to my chest. We made out for a minute, furtively, roughly, among the trombones and French horns. When he pulled away, he spoke before I could. Don't tell anyone about this, he said, and I didn't.

What evidence would you present?

EXHIBIT 1: Here I am, frozen in front of her locked bedroom door. Picture, ladies and gentlemen, that window of time when a girl is at her most awkward. Breast buds protruding, braces gnashing into mouth flesh, smile like Goofy (I don't know yet not to smile), always looking, looking, looking at everyone, in their eyes, trying to Make. A. Connection.

After my mother finally confessed her affair and the pregnancy that came of it, when my youngest brother was just beginning to toddle, the suburban house with the cursive *Twenty-Four* scrawled above the garage door was sold and the three of us children moved into the city with my mother (now called a "single mother"). She was madly in love with her lover and wanted him to marry her. Once or twice a week he would visit, in between runs down the ski slopes and adventure trips to the Amazon; he would hold his toddler, cradle him, bring him gifts.

I took care of my brothers while she made her case to him. I tried not to listen, but sometimes I stopped in front of her locked bedroom door, unable to move or to reconcile the sounds of the body that, at twelve, I knew but didn't want to think I did. A testimony of sorts: That she had what he wanted, what it would take to make him happy. That she, all of us, were good enough. That our first family had disintegrated for a reason, so that this family could work. She plead her case behind a closed bedroom door, and I bore witness.

When you are asked to state We are a family, why don't you?

I sometimes find it helpful to think of Angerona, or Angeronia, a Roman divinity with seemingly conflicting identities. According to some evidence she is the goddess of pain and sorrow, anguish and fear, the one who could relieve men of these states. Other accounts frame Angerona as the goddess of silence, whose role in Rome was to prevent the sacred name of the city from being uttered and thus made known to enemies. Some describe her as the one who was tasked with helping sustain men through the dark, hard days of winter. Her statue stood in the temple of Volupia, near the porta Romanula and the Forum, and she was represented with her mouth bound and sealed up, which according to Massurius Sabinus indicated that those who hid their anxiety in patience would attain the greatest joy. A festival, Angeronalia, was celebrated in Rome in honor of Angerona every year on December 21, when the pontiffs offered sacrifices to her in the temple of Volupia.

Did you hear that? The goddess of silence was placed inside the temple of the goddess of pleasure.

Where does their failure end and yours begin?

Adultery, from the Latin *adulterare*. Adulteration, same family.

accident   adversity   affliction   bane blemish   blow   breakage

bruise casualty   catastrophe   cave-in   contamination corruption

debasement   depreciation   deprivation   destruction

deterioration   detriment   devastation   disservice   disturbance ~~evil~~ no

one here is evil   falsify   hardship   harm   hurt

illness   impairment   infliction

knockout   marring   mischief

mishap   mutilation

outrage   pollution   ravage

reverse   ruin

is our ruin my fault?   spoilage

stroke   suffering

waste

wound

wreckage

What are you asking for, an imaginary redo?

STATE YOUR NAME FOR THE RECORD.

Fuck. You.

Some witnesses feel it helps to reimagine their experience as another's

I think about Pearl, whose mother, Hester, invited the devil himself into her body when she pursued earthly pleasures instead of obeying and truly fearing the Lord. Did Hester envision the plucky, bawling Pearl when she spread her creamy thighs for the Reverend Dimmesdale?

Regardless of intent, Pearl took shape, microscopic scarlet letter-A cells arising from the secret matter of life.

Would the child Pearl be able to take the stand and testify, convincingly and for all her decriers to witness, We are a family?

We have as yet hardly spoken of the infant.

JUDGE: State your name for the record.

PEARL: Pearl Prynne.

JUDGE, *frowning*: Is thou as whorish as thy mother?

PEARL: Why dost thou smile at me so?

JUDGE: Thy spirit pleaseth me, child. I will see you now in my chambers.

WITNESSES, *whispering*: If the hussy stood up for judgment before us five, that are now here in a knot together, would she come off with such a sentence?

Would you prefer we call character witnesses?

JUDGE: Did any of you engage in any sexual acts with this girl, the daughter of an adulteress?

JAY K.: When we were eleven Natalie said she would be my girlfriend. At a party in December in Cara's basement we slow danced to Berlin and I kissed her but the bitch wouldn't let me put my tongue in. Then she broke up with me and I told her she lost her chance, I would never go out with her ever again.

DAVID R.: I think we made out a few times in the band room. I actually had a girlfriend at the time, so this wasn't, like, a thing. It was never going to lead anywhere. Sweet girl, though. Great legs.

JONATHAN C.: I love that kid, she's just cool, you know? Once we hung out and she gave me a hand job. At first I was confused because she was like really rubbing up and down frantically. I thought maybe it was her first time. But I helped her along and it was all good.

OLDER STAFF COUNSELOR AT SLEEPAWAY CAMP: I never rubbed my hands up under a camper's shirt while we sat by the fire on a five-day canoe trip, whatareyoufuckingtalkingabout?

JEFF, OLDER COUNSELOR OF HER YOUNGER BROTHER: I thought she had some balls for sneaking out that night. We went on a short walk. Another night I took her downtown on the metro. We kissed. I definitely fingered her pussy, just really gave it to her no holds barred. After a few minutes she said, Okay, that's all you get and actually just walked herself home. And I was like, That's all *I* get?! Bitches are crazy.

ADAM G.: I thought about dating her every day of my life for two years. I wanted to marry her. I knew I'd eventually become prime minister of Canada and I thought she would make the perfect wife. I loved everything about her. But she always saw me as only a friend, I guess. One summer when I confessed to her I was in love with her, she gasped in disbelief.

JASON: Her mind is like a diamond mine. I could kiss her forever. We went to half of third base, I guess you would say. I held her in my arms. I licked her nipples like they were warm maple syrup drizzled on a bank of February snow. Once we were making out in the closet at a friend's house and she started moaning and I knew she wanted me to, um, go down on her. And I did for like a minute or two but I don't think I was ready. She seemed a little frustrated after that. But later I gave her her first orgasm and I think I saw tears in her eyes.

What evidence would you present?

EXHIBIT 2: When my mother became a single mother, she went to work. My baby brother went to daycare. In the mornings when I was eleven, I helped bundle up my middle brother, Steven, and walk with him to the corner of the street where we would wait for the school bus to take us to first and sixth grades.

One January morning the Montreal sky was a smutty gray and the cold bit through our woolen mittens. My brother dug the tip of his boot into a sticky snowdrift at the edge of the icy sidewalk. I looked across the road and saw a man standing alone near the side yard of a neighbor's house. He was dressed in a brown trench coat and boots. Our eyes met in gaps between the traffic of cars and slush-covered city buses. He looked at me with one hand in his pocket. I watched silently as he opened his trench coat with his other hand, reached down, opened the fly of his pants, and brought out his penis.

Of course, he didn't tell me not to tell anyone. But I didn't.

What does this have to do with anything?

Because I could not speak, because I could not say, when interrogated in that courtroom, We are a family—because women have bodies that can lead to the unraveling of everything—we lost my little brother. He was put on a plane and flown away from the sunset, back to Montreal and the smug safety of his father who had, rather suddenly, forfeited the Amazon trips for a new wife. The happy couple—better than us, more whole than us, a fresh slate—was quickly working to manufacture even more babies of their own.

My mother's reaction to this tear in the space-time continuum was an unrelenting howl that made the palm trees behind our California dream home shudder in the night.

When do things unravel?

As fall gave way to a mild and sunny winter, shiny shopping bags piled up and things became uncomfortable inside the California house. Our parents fought more, and I knew from my mother's whispered confessions that, whereas before she had tolerated it, she now couldn't stand having sex with Josef. At least twice a week my mother slipped into my bed instead of going to sleep in the master suite. This did not sit well with my step-father, who barked more and pulled the previously loose purse strings tighter. When she wasn't sobbing, my mother grew defiant, taking passive-aggressive actions like cooking every meal with cheese when Asher could not stand cheese.

I forgot, she said, as she set down another oozing casserole or four-cheese pizza.

But mainly, the proxy targets for the growing disharmony were the pets. We (my mother and brothers) were not cat people. You are or you aren't—these things go back generations. Loyalty and allegiance must lie with one species only. We were dog people, always had been, always would be. Any ownership of cats was accidental and non-memorable.

Josef and his sons were cat. Into the marriage they brought Perky, a tiny gray thing. Often Asher could be found stretched out on the carpet, limbs akimbo, communing with Perky.

Into the marriage we brought Brandy, a neurotic poodle that my mother especially adored. Sometimes my mother thought Brandy looked so cute that she cooed at him like a baby, applying her favorite love name, Shmushy. At first Josef just teasingly disliked Brandy, who used to sleep snuggled into my mother's bed every night, until they married and he was relocated to my bed. Josef joked that maybe Brandy would get accidentally thrown out with the trash or run over by the car, then wink at my mother. It was the early days of polite step-family tolerance; we laughed nervously.

But then, the jokes became violent.

Stupid little fucking shit! sneered Josef as he walked by Brandy on his way to the kitchen.

Sometimes, he'd jut his leg out toward the dog or make a thick fist and punch the air a few feet above the dog's curly white head. Brandy took to cowering any time Josef walked past, and despite elaborate security measures taken by my mother and me to lock Brandy in my bedroom when we both left the house, we worried what danger he might be in when we weren't around. We had never actually seen Josef hit anyone or anything, but we weren't stupid: he had boasted about being in the Six-Day War.

In retaliation we did what we could to publicly dislike the innocent, non-memorable Perky. Weird animal, my mother or I would snort as we passed by the soft, gray lump sitting on the couch. We tried, but the insults came out half-hearted, deflated of any real animosity. It was hard to peg your frustrations on an indifferent, seven-pound cat that minds its own business.

What does the end look like?

Just after the new year, when tension in the house was at its height, we got a call from my Uncle Jon.

So, I'm gay, he revealed, his voice shaky. I don't want to live a lie anymore. I'm moving to California.

My mother and I were overjoyed. She asked all kinds of inappropriate, weirdly probing questions (How do you know who goes on top?). Then we waited impatiently to have company out West. Jon arrived in early spring, with a new job as a financial executive, to sleep on our couch until he found a place of his own.

All of a sudden, Josef could leave Brandy the dog alone because there was a new target in town.

What is this fucking shit? Josef muttered as we strolled, on another family outing, down the sidewalks of San Francisco's Castro District. We had traveled there to visit the city's historic gay neighborhood, which had been, up until now, overlooked in the family tourism oeuvre. We had promised to help Jon find somewhere to live.

Men were everywhere: thick, burly bearded men; tiny, tidy men; many-tattooed men; tall, golden airbrushed men; men in boots, heels, nerdy white knee socks with royal blue athletic stripes, and no clothes at all. They strolled unhurriedly in pairs, hands squeezed into each other's back pockets; sported gold lamé shorts and nipple rings; kissed each other hello and goodbye in covered doorways; popped in and out of the sex-toy shops and book stores; laughed from patio tables underneath the lush vegetation of outdoor cafés.

Rainbow flags rippled from the ice-cream-hued Victorian

homes that snaked up the hills. The local theater marquis announced an upcoming live drag tribute to Elizabeth Taylor, Get Your Tickets Now! The antique emerald streetcar squeaked and sighed to a stop on the corner of Market and Castro, letting off more men and picking up others. A few women dotted the landscape, hanging with the gay guys or wrapped up in each other. Everyone seemed chill, convivial, friendly, familial.

Who knew, my mother exclaimed.

Jon looked nervous but happy. I was fascinated. Here was a whole population of people saying Screw it to outside expectations, creating a world of their own. People living the way they wanted to, anything and everything for the taking, fuck convention. This was the essence of the California I'd been hoping for, I realized, even if I hadn't exactly been able to envision it before. We could all use more freedom like this. Let freedom reign!

We are leaving right now, Josef ordered us just then. He looked, for once, despite his thick, six-foot-four frame, like he was shrinking. Get back to the car, he snarled, apparently pushed over the edge by one pair of gold butt cheeks too many. Jon, he barked, you can find somewhere to live on your own.

How ugly will it get?

Would you shut up? my mother hisses at Josef one night in March, while Jon is in the bathroom washing up. Josef had wondered aloud whether he should warn the neighbors that we have a "pretty boy" in our house who might be trying to spy on their naked husbands through the nighttime windows.

Hey, he barks at all of us, this is my house. He reaches for the control and switches the TV from a documentary on whales to his favorite show, *Home Improvement*, where the maligned father with a penchant for tools makes stupid man jokes over a fence.

I was watching that, I snip, and grab the controller back.

Fuck off! shrieks Asher from the armchair in the corner of the den, banging the channel up button directly on the TV box back to *Home Improvement*.

Freak!

Bitch!

You're all crazy, Ric mutters from inside his video game.

ALL OF YOU SHUT UP! bellows Josef, just as Jon walks in holding his toothbrush, facial moisturizer, and a *New Yorker*.

Don't talk to them like that, my uncle says in a very cool way.

I WILL SPEAK HOWEVER I WANT TO IN MY HOUSE AND IF YOU DON'T LIKE IT YOU CAN LEAVE!

Duly noted, Jon says, almost cattily, and the room clears, all units retreating to their safe zones.

By the time Jon does leave our couch, no one is speaking to anyone not related to them by blood. My mother is stashing grocery money "for a rainy day." Meals are silent. Ridiculous gripes float to the surface: Can whoever opens the goddamn mailbox close it after themselves, Josef demands; Who left that bathroom fan on, screeches my mother.

I give her the best advice I can: get us the hell out of here.

I am drifting like a dinghy from my former life. Jason and I are not together anymore, but my acrylic nails shine, my hair has taken on a sun-tinted golden hue, and though I am lonely I imagine that intelligent and fun future friends and boyfriends are just around the corner.

I'm seventeen. I will be able to move out on my own soon. All I have to do right now is hang on until something shakes us fully loose into our real American dream.

**Sometimes a polygraph or other forensic test
is used to detect lies**

One afternoon can look just like all the others except when you come home and find Perky the cat curled up on the carpet in your room. Strange because she never comes into your room—she knows you're dog.

You pick up a clean ball of socks from the laundry pile and toss it at her. The balled-up socks hit her coat and bounce right off, but Perky doesn't budge.

You tiptoe closer and slowly reach out your pointer finger toward her downy charcoal head. When you touch it, you shriek and pull back. Stiff! This cat is very, very stiff.

You have never touched a dead body before, but you know that is what Perky is. Dead in your bedroom. A weird panic overtakes you, your mouth flies open and you are mute for a moment before you start to scream. You scream and scream and scream until, finally, people come running.

The step-family thinks you killed her. There are grim, closed-door consultations and looks of death from Asher to you. Your step-father orders an actual cat autopsy to make sure there has been no foul play. All members of the house take sides, aligning themselves cleanly by clan.

A week later the autopsy report shows death by natural causes, but your transformation is already underway. Really, it began a long time ago, when you first filed onto that westbound plane.

The seams had already begun to pop, and now the threads rip fast. The for sale sign, the same one that awaited you all when you first came to California, is hammered back into the pink house's manicured lawn. Moving boxes are pulled out of the barely unpacked garage and packed again. Family advisors are consulted, go-aheads given, accounts divided. Two separate apartments are leased, one for them and one for you. No one seems surprised.

By late spring, a year and a half after you first arrive, the two sides of your makeshift family are divided so permanently that none of you will ever see the other side again.

Blood, it turns out, is thicker than water. Cut the chaff, move ahead.

The truth is already becoming clear to you: To fully assimilate, you need to dissolve. In order to let California absorb you, you can no longer pretend to belong to each other. There is room for only one master. You have only to fracture, to let go of one façade in exchange for another. Some things must be lost so that you may achieve higher gains. And anyway, you did this one thing together—you redirected your fates.

You have chosen your allegiances. None are to each other. But that's okay.

California calls.

PART FOUR

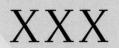

What happens after everything has been washed away?

With the step-family and my little brother gone, I was clear to lead an emotionless life. Nothing could be turned around, so I would have to find a home inside nothing and make it something.

What could you not let go of?

That something was wrong with me. That I harbored in me deficiencies, some inborn broken thing that would stop me from everything. That would stop me from looking up and around, from asking how this is done. That burned my neck and cheeks red when it was my turn to speak in a college class or on the street, in a checkout line, ordering a sandwich, anywhere I was not with only myself. That grabbed my breath, hauled the breathing right out of me like some kind of phantom riding a dark horse in a children's fairy tale. That stood between me and the man I wanted to touch, the ones I wanted to touch—there were more than one. An obstruction to integrating. I could not let go of the fault of my shortcomings, failed opportunities, silent conversations and missed connections. Anxiety that never ended, a roller coaster stuck in the on position. I could not coerce myself into believing this wasn't because of something wrong with me from the start, or something I carried with me.

Be careful what you wish for

I remember something else about the burden of silence. Once when I was seven or eight and living in the *Twenty-Four* house, I grew angry at my mother. Maybe she had yelled at me for some disobedience—possibly I talked back to her or did not pick up my toys, or had taken too long getting into my pajamas after supper and bath time, when she must have been out of her mind to get children to bed and for an hour or two be able to breathe. Maybe she had spanked me, a normal spanking or one where the boundary between punishment and fury blurred into a dangerous static like some of the far-flung television stations past channel 58, where I had to click, click, click, click to find *The Twilight Zone*.

In my bedroom, where I might have sequestered myself or been sent, I felt terrible for myself and thought furious thoughts about my mother, and as I settled into this preoccupation my mind began to wander more loosely, faster and faster into uncharted territory. I recalled a recent episode of *The Twilight Zone* I had seen on a Saturday morning while the sky was still dark and I snuck down into the living room for the types of shows like this that aired before cartoons began. The episode was titled "The Children's Zoo," and in it a little girl has parents who fight a lot and yell at her. Fed up, the girl gives her parents an invitation she receives that reads: "As bearer of this special invitation, you are entitled to one child's admission to the CHILDREN'S ZOO. You will be offered all the special privileges described by the other girl who passed this." As the girl begins to tour the zoo herself, we, the TV viewers, see that it is not animals inside the cages but parents, and the children who visit are being given the chance to choose a new set of parents to leave with.

In the episode, the girl soon spots her own parents, outraged and horrible, trapped behind observation glass. Though she has the power, in the end she refuses to save them, choosing another mother and father instead. Snuggled under a blanket on our couch, my eyes had widened as the story came to its climax: *Relinquish your parents?* I thought. *Was that done?*

Now banished to my bedroom, I imagined the zoo with my mother behind her own slab of thick glass, and before I could stop my brain a brand new word I had never even flirted with surfaced: fuck. Two words, actually. *Fuck you*, I spat silently in my head, to my mother. *Fuck. You.* And though the words did not emerge from my lips, they had been in the room. They had been conjured, meaning, I believed, that I spoke them all the same. Immediately, a panic seeped through me. *What have I done? How could I have even thought it? What terrible thing will happen now?*

I could live with the guilt for all of five minutes. I opened my bedroom door, raced down the carpeted stairs two at a time and planted myself in front of my mother, who sat next to my father watching *Dallas* on TV. She looked at me, mildly annoyed. What is it? she asked.

I said something, I stuttered, Something about you. In my head, I said … I said … a bad thing … *fff* … it was, I didn't, I'm sorry …

The tears began to come and I squinted my eyes, trying to decide whether she had received the message I was trying to convey.

Okay, honey, she said, her eyes flickering back to the screen, where J. R. was raging. My father snorted.

Go to bed now, my mother offered evenly, in finality, unconcerned, or still ignorant, or benevolent about the transgression I had just attempted to confess.

What did I learn from this confession, I ask myself.

A story is yours alone until it is spoken. When words are secret, it is you who decides if they exist.

But why are you silenced?

I have an attraction to escape stories, to reinvention narratives, tales of Amish, Orthodox, and polygamist girls, of girls locked in attics, ushering in their own freedom, heisting it. What am I trying to escape from, to hasten?

I am afraid of not belonging, of there being no place right for me.

I am afraid of becoming attached to things that go away. To people who are reassigned.

I am afraid of it being discovered that I do not belong. The writer Mattilda Bernstein Sycamore calls it the search for things that don't unravel in the end.

Silence is a disappearance. Disappearance is an erasure.

The response to my exploitation is a self-erasure.

The response to interrogation is a question returned.

At college what will you be afraid to say?

Excuse me—
What's your major?
Where is the humanities building?
A side of salsa, please.
What are your office hours?
Do you want to study together?
I don't want to fuck you.
I'm lost.
(I'm lonely.)
I'm failing biology.
I'm failing history.
I miss my brother.
I'm failing.
Sometimes I almost fall asleep driving down the highway.
I want you to fuck me.
I'm falling.

Tell us the truth

Longing is embedded in belonging, hidden in plain sight. To desire openly—to desire after a silencing—is to strip to the skin and lie in the street for the crowd, rocks in hand, to see.

Later, when I am a young student journalist covering city council meetings about building permits and parking fees, I will dream about placing myself in real danger. I consider doing the work it would take to become a foreign correspondent. I long to embed myself with a military troupe—it would not be that hard to arrange—to disguise myself poorly and head into the heart of enemy territory, surrounded by bodies of tension, by ranks of unsecured need.

Tell us the real truth

I am afraid to do this in front of everyone.

Are you Californian yet?

I have a boyfriend now. I meet him at the end of my senior year in high school. I am in need of a group or, really, any human connection, but I have entered the realm of American high school far too late to form deep and selective friendships. So I allow myself to drift along with a somewhat welcoming cluster of kids who are generally interested in privation: They are members of DARE, making pledges in AA-like group circles not to drink alcohol or do drugs. Some of the girls flash a gold band on their right ring finger, slipped on them by their fathers in a special ceremony and representing their pledge to remain virgins until marriage. The rings repulse me and also force me to think of my own father, whom I haven't spoken with since I left for California. Our relationship has been strained since I was fourteen, when he remarried to a woman who disliked me and took on a seven-year-old step-daughter. It feels like I am always on the outside, the daughter who reminds everyone of her mother (and so what?). Tainted.

I don't know what it is that draws me to Jim—he's a generally kind person but we are not well matched. His interest in me is probably what determines our courtship, because I am inept at deciphering my own desires or preferences. He's a member of DARE, too, but he is learning to manage the guilt of indulgences like beer and shooting fuel-tank levels of Jagermeister. His family is Episcopalian; a reference to the Lord or Jesus could pop any time from his mother's mouth or from some longtime friend in Jim's clean-cut, Nascar-loving circle of boyhood friends, though Jim himself is moving into a loosening. In April, before we begin dating, I am invited to the family's Easter dinner. Sitting before the first glazed ham I have ever seen up close, I mention that because I am Jewish the finer points of Easter are unfamiliar to me. Jim's mother, Anne, who I will soon learn maintains a special room in their home just for storing her abundant collection of decorations for Christmas, Easter, St. Patrick's Day, St. Valentine's Day, and other such holidays, looks worriedly at Jim as her eyes tear up. I'm not sure I can have someone at my Easter table who doesn't believe in the Lord Jesus Christ, she says softly.

This reminds me of a cowboy at my high school, a senior with a palm-sized belt buckle and a chipped front tooth named Sean who earlier this winter took me for a couple of rides in his gray pickup truck. After the last ride, we parked in front of my house and I bumped my head as we kissed chastely on the lips. While pulling away he noticed the tiny gold Jewish star dangling around my neck. What is that, he wanted to know. I told him. The cowboy never asked me out again. Later, away from the cramped chamber of that cab, I wished I had had the chance to run my tongue one time along the tooth's sharp edge.

But now I'm with Jim, and Jim has a car, a Mustang he diligently saved for by mowing summer lawns, and with him I begin to see the California beyond our suburbs. It will become a hallmark of our relationship, perhaps the very purpose of it: a joint desire, though possibly for different reasons, to venture out, trace our fingers along a paper map and then together move our bodies to that place. To constellate ourselves by crossing over to somewhere new, to bear witness to what is there.

Draw a map of your heart

MONTEREY

Witness: Air that is shampoo of wet salt, lathers my long hair into a sea sponge, foamy spa scrub, weapon to whip the cheeks.

Witness: Sand is not sand is the gentlest burial.

Witness: You take a spoon to your lips. A warm sweet sidles in, molten clam cream.

Witness: Motel 6, sodden towel crumple, sheets that smell of … sea.

Draw a map of your body

Jim's parents owned a small yacht. Every couple of weekends we went aboard, small bags of essentials packed, for a short cruising trip through the California Delta or along the Sacramento River. Jim's older sister, Lee-Anne, who went to a nearby community college and struggled with a mild failure-to-launch problem, came with her thirty-something boyfriend, Nick, and for a couple of days we grilled burgers, played cards and watched for herons. Sometimes Jim's father spread out his nautical charts, traced his finger along their hair-thin green and blue lines, cryptic numbers, keys and curves, and tried to show me how to navigate.

At night LeeAnne and I slept in the pilot house bed, while Jim and Nick crashed in the main cabin, on the dining table and couch that transformed, with the sigh of a hydraulic lever, into beds, because Jim's parents wanted to ensure no sex outside of wedlock happened on their watch.

One Saturday, we planned to motor up to a place called Snug Harbor. The boat, *Chug*, was slow, and once we navigated out of the marina, the quiet swallows of the engine and the slight waves of the jungle-like water could lull you into a sort of awake meditation. Jim, Nick, and Jim's dad discussed sports. His mother and LeeAnne began to prepare a spaghetti dinner in the tiny galley. Outside, the autumn sun was bleeding closer to the glassy edge of bobbing horizon. I quietly excused myself to the bathroom.

In the tiny head, I shut the thin levered door, leaned against the circular sink mounted into its polished teak cabinet and lifted my leg onto the toilet seat. I rubbed myself softly at first, then harder, trying not to make a sound, trying not to laugh, not to cry, until after a few minutes the swell of relief I was desperate for came through me like a flood and I closed my eyes and bit my lip not to scream. Through the bathroom's porthole the California sunset poured like ruby.

You seem to enjoy pushing the envelope

Once Suzanne dared me to read the book *Twilight*. I had been making fun of her obsession with it. We both knew it wasn't real literature. I know, she said, but you'll see, once you start reading it you are hooked. She offered to give me $10, all I had to do was read the book. In *Twilight*, werewolf Jacob Black is subjected to a process known as imprinting, the involuntary mechanism by which Quileute shapeshifters find their mates. It is a gravitational pull; an unconditional binding.

> It's not like love at first sight, really. It's more like … gravity moves … suddenly. It's not the earth holding you here anymore, she does … You become whatever she needs you to be, whether that's a protector, or a lover, or a friend.
>
> —JACOB BLACK, explaining to Bella Swan about imprinting

In psychology and ethology, imprinting is any kind of phase-sensitive learning that is rapid and apparently independent of the consequences of behavior. Imprinting is hypothesized to have a critical period—a maturational stage in the lifespan of an organism during which the nervous system is especially sensitive to certain environmental stimuli.

This explains everything about my relationship with California as I assimilated into myself.

I was falling in love.

I was being cut loose.

I was floating away.

Who were your friends?

While we still lived in the house with Josef, some people I knew from Montreal came to visit me, two counselors who had taken care of me while I was a teenager at sleepaway camp, both named Warren, and two girls they were traveling with. The Warrens had been my counselors when I was fifteen and sixteen. I was seventeen now and they were in their early twenties. They were all on a road trip across the West and they needed to find free places to stay as often as possible. My mother was out of town, and Josef did not disguise how irritated he was by four slightly dirty young people camped out on our living room floor's pink carpet.

I wanted badly to make a good impression on the Warrens, to connect to them on this special stopover of theirs that was reuniting us three thousand miles from where we had known each other. They had both guided me through many little dramas during camp summers, and for a while I had also believed I was in love with one of them. For two summers and the year in between while I still lived in Montreal, I had thrown myself at this particular Warren, trying all my girly wiles to get him to cross a line between mentor/friend into something more that I thought I was dying for. Steadfastly, often grinning and groaning at my pleas for a kiss, he gently rebuffed me, slinging an arm in a counselor-like way around my shoulders and feeding me facts about his band idols—The Cure, Pink Floyd, Phish— so I could at least be filled by his musical knowledge.

The other Warren had written me dependably that past year, my first in California, responding to my sometimes-panicked letters worrying over the perfect high school girls and my longing for Jason back home, delivering brotherly advice in upper case block script.

In California, though, the foursome was already knotted tightly from their weeks traveling together, united by inside jokes from the uninhibited freedom of crisscrossing countries of their own wills. As I toured them down San Francisco's Haight Street, pointing out the historic head shops and larger-than-life corners that had stood sentinel over hippies and flower children during the Summer of Love, I felt more childlike than ever, on the outside. With their patched backpacks and relaxed postures, they strode the San Francisco sidewalks with a comfort I never could settle into. If I couldn't feel at home in a group or with my family, at least I wanted to be enmeshed in a place, in this city, my state; I yearned for an ease and facility I could show off and be possessed by, as though California herself were living up to all of my expectations and anticipations, my most intimate partner, the prize that bears out.

Instead I functioned awkwardly for a few days, the kid sister, tagging along to narrate and point the Warrens and their traveling companions to fog-shrouded beaches and cheap burritos, and then we parted ways with hugs as they drove off into their futures and I stood in my place on the sidewalk waving and squinting into the sky.

What did you see in him?

It's a startling little box that can tether you hook, line, and sinker to a person. Through the vibrating plastic you feel the elastic tendons of connection alight with energy. Numbers now mean letters; secret messages are cloaked in mathematical upside-downness. Later you will be forced to strain, not unlike the elastic of your attachment, to remember which numbers meant what message: 666 is *I want to fuck,* yes? Or is it just the devil as it has always been? Some inverted numbers buzz through to say h-E-L-L-O. There is a code for *How's your day?* One, maybe, for *I love you*—something to do with an E? 69 is frequently employed, the thrill of sending these particular numbers across this invisible new message highway more arousing than any real live act that might in fact result from the signal. How capable you think men with pagers attached prominently to their waists, to their leather belts, look, ready for absolutely anything that could arise, able to synch with you no matter the distance, to speak to you independent of voice. A tool, too, to regulate power: a page from someone else, other than "your" man, might come in while you two are together. A silent glance at your hot pink or oxide gray box in its hard, matching shell—the one he in fact bought for you—can say so much: your receptors are open for any and all incoming messages; the airwaves are crackling with competition; your signal is on and strong. Later, many years later, decades, you will occasionally bolt awake at night in panic. Soaked in sweat, even. Your fear, taking shape in a dream, slamming into the state of waking, is this: you want to page him, you *must page him right now,* but no matter what you do you cannot remember his number.

What if your relationship with Jim was presented as flash fiction?

We are going to the Applebee's. We are taking his truck, the gray Mazda pickup. Or is it the white Mustang with maroon leather seats and a tail fin? "The 5-Oh," he calls it, often with baby at the end. "5-Oh, BABY!" He picks me up at the curb and we cruise, windows down, past the four-bedroom two-and-a-half-bath plus master soaking tubs and the five-bedroom chef's kitchen custom closet plus bonus game rooms. The roads are pretty clear tonight, even with all the V8 leather seat 20″ alloy wheels heading home from work. I lean in across the bench to deliver a kiss to his smooth cheek. He has a new pair of Nikes on. "WHAT'S GOIN DOWN, GIRL? LET'S GET THIS PARTY STARTED!" Applebee's is not far from our houses, just a few minutes on Camino Ramon past the Target Greatland, Caspers Hot Dogs, Ross Dress for Less, T.J. Maxx where you never miss a designer deal, two Taco Bells featuring for a limited time ninety-nine-cent flavor-blasted chalupas, Bishop Ranch Business Park I, Bishop Ranch Business Park II, Bishop Ranch Business Park III, and Bishop Ranch Business Park IV.

> there's going to be a
> heartache
> tonight

He works undercover security at the Target, hiding in the clothing racks and spying on bored housewives who steal lingerie. His favorite thing is when they cry in his office. "I take them down and the first thing every single one does is start blubbering. DANG, it's hilarious!" he tells me and his parents and sister over burger barbecues on the weekends, lifting another Mountain Dew from the cooler. "All they care about is that I don't call their husbands. 'My husband's going to divorce me, please, I'll do anything, I'm begging you.' Shoulda thought of that before, KLEPTO!"

cut that out, or
I'll really give you something
to cry about

We pull into the parking lot and walk into the Applebee's. Some of his friends are already there at the table, the dude who's also in the junior volunteer police officer training academy; the guy who went to the high school and now does … something; that one guy who country line dances. Plus some of their girlfriends, big eyelashes on the menu. Also on the menu, a glossy brochure with detailed close-ups: green bean crispers, crosscut double glazed wonton riblets, Inca fusion nachos, and supersized Bahama Mama with commemorative take-home Big Fister™ cup. I order a chef salad. I think tonight will be the night. His parents are away for the weekend on their boat, *Chug*. I've been waiting but it feels like the time to do it. His bedroom is the same as when he was a kid, with a mini Nerf basketball hoop on the back of the door and cowboy sheets. Except now he keeps his Beretta under the bed, in a locked box. For academy training. But maybe, since his parents are away, we would do it in the living room on the floor in front of the fireplace. His mom is a quilter; she makes huge artistic scenes hand-pieced together, tugboats jostling with the sea in a storm; kittens pawing yarn; fresh, dewy tulips. The quilts hang on the wall by the fireplace and his father's collection of beer and firefighting memorabilia. It does seem like tonight is the time to do it. It would be weird to hold off any longer. "RIGHT ON, GIRL!" Anyway, here come the riblets.

stop while you're ahead, no
regrets

You had wanted Jason to do it?

I had loved him in a way that I will always be able to slip into. On a trip back to Montreal ten months after moving to California, just after I turned seventeen and as our romance-in-letters was winding down, I asked him directly. I want it to be you, is what I said. He held me in his arms, slipped his tongue around mine, sent a torrent of need straight to the splitting middle of me, and told me, that sweet boy, No. He thought we weren't ready.

What would the Prynne girl do?

Sometimes, suspended in a state of longing, you can only refer to the characters who have been presented to you, whom you appropriate—perhaps from the pages of texts that help you navigate California and yourself in it, perhaps from the topography around you—in hopes that a mirror, however distorted, could lead to a sense of satiety.

I often think about Pearl, birthed by her author in the year of California's Gold Rush. As a toddler and young girl she believes fiercely, without any public evidence to support the notion, that she should be adored. Later, she asks Dimmesdale and her mother when she will be acknowledged fully and, given no certainties, demands it. Against all conventions, Pearl exposes her own longing, does not shy from insisting that she be seen and therefore written into existence. Asking questions, then, is a kind of granting of permission to oneself, an entering into a state of permissiveness. Interrogation is a taking possession of one's being. A (re) claiming of voice.

I think Pearl would want to tour the shit out of California and, for a little while, bide her time.

What is this difficulty you have with the word *alien*?

During the summer after my first year in California, I rode around in Jim's Mustang and climbed grassy suburban hills above winking subdivisions, where I sat with other teenage couples and my boyfriend's fingers tickling my crotch to watch the night moon suspended in the scattered haze of urban lights. Above a ridge in Livermore, a town that functioned as a boundary between the easternmost reaches of the San Francisco Bay Area's urbanish core and the farther East Bay's still rural carpet of ranches and hillocks rolling toward the Sierras, I squinted in the direction of Lawrence Livermore Laboratory. Before our family exploded, my step-father Josef had told us of this lab, where American nuclear warheads had been designed and guarded since the Cold War.

These places of hard science, where equations and formulas held the secrets of life, felt both unknowable and entrancing. In nearby Mountain View, I knew that people paid to believe in extraterrestrial life babysat interstellar message machinery at the SETI Institute (SETI standing for the search for extraterrestrial intelligence). For years they waited patiently, the scientists, watching for a sign that something was out there, beyond our known human sphere. Two decades later I would read that, no longer satisfied with just waiting and listening to their equipment for a message from beyond to finally arrive from its years-long galactic journey, scientists had decided to mobilize into "active SETI," beaming out intentional messages for aliens through radar and, they soon hoped, lasers. The scientists, finally, found their voice.

I thought about the documents in my manila folder, all stamped "alien." About the Montreal I once knew so well that I could smell the year's first snow on the air hours before it fell. About my father and his new family driving to a Sunday-night, Chinese-food dinner on Queen Mary Avenue, traveling now on a separate trajectory. About Jason, the way his drumsticks rocketed across the surface of his drums; the mysterious blue mark hidden on a soft, inside part of his skin. I believed other versions of life existed, besides these, a belief buoyed by the stories I had read as a child in my *Into the Unknown* book about spaceship sightings, powerful fetish objects, and other unexplained phenomena. Was someone, something, watching me right now from some other dimension, I puzzled, as Jim's fingers paused their orbiting to slip beneath the waistband of my leggings.

What would Mary Ann do?

I skipped a year of high school when we arrived in California, so even though I just barely turned seventeen, I attend San Francisco State University now. I am still living with my mother and Steven in the suburbs, forty-five minutes east. I don't know why I don't leave, go live in the city in a crumbly, grand Victorian with seven roommates, ride Muni and trolleys around instead of commuting hours in my car over bridges and across the bay to get to my classes; why I don't move to where I could walk every night to loud dark clubs and swallow the bright liquids that would make me forget my schoolwork, the fear that I carry around during the day but don't understand, that would permit me to get lost. I want to leave, maybe I want to, but I am scared. Maybe I am tethered to Jim, who lives around the corner with his parents and goes to community college, who represents playing it safe. Or tethered to my mother, who dates bad matches and works in the front office of a mortgage company and tallies her checkbook worriedly at the dining table. One morning I wake up and move toward the kitchen of our small apartment, where I find a man I have never seen before, shirtless, black hair matted, rummaging through our fridge. Got any orange juice? he asks me. Hello, I say slowly, I live here—who are you? I let my annoyance infect my words (my mother later apologizes—You're right, you're right, she says, that wasn't safe), but inside I am conducting a panicked self-inquiry: am I pissed because there's a stranger in our house or because I'm jealous? Maybe I want to be the one waking with a strange man in my bed.

At college I am required to take History of San Francisco. We read the works of Norris and Ferlinghetti and Armistead Maupin's *Tales of The City*, books that, while being absent of female voices like mine, nevertheless permit me to situate myself in the parade of characters who have come to California and this city searching for something.

At first I am excited about Mary Ann Singleton, the twenty-something secretary in *Tales* who arrives in San Francisco from Cleveland for a vacation and decides on impulse to stay. Mary Ann is naïve, sheltered, but she knows this and wants to break out of her shell. She finds an apartment at 28 Barbary Lane, where she becomes enmeshed with a cast of archetypes—a pot-growing landlady; a bisexual patchouli-oil-spritzing hippie; a sweet, girl's-best-friend gay guy; a dysfunctional chauvinist businessman; etc.

Eventually, by the end of the book, Mary Ann is annoying. She picks the wrong guys. She underestimates her career potential. She's timid. She gets very stuck, at least in this first of Maupin's many soap operaish installments. It worries me.

So what again is the issue?

Most of the hours I spend at my thirty thousand-student college I am silent. I am afraid to speak. My skin prickles when I walk into the cafeteria. I only go there, among all the strangers, because I need to eat. I want to make friends, but when my body moves into a public space I become aware that everyone is watching me. It is difficult to breathe most days. Illogically, I feel sixty thousand eyes on me. I don't tell a single person about this dull terror that hardly ever leaves me, and for a long time I never will.

How can I put this more simply? In public I cannot open my mouth.

Every time I have to open my mouth in public to speak, it feels like I am on a witness stand. My chest tightens and a heat crawls up my neck. Even when I am asked something as simple as my name, it seems like I am being asked to account for everything that is.

Silence, examined

EXHIBIT 1A: Qualities of sound and color

Once on a night after I was fully grown I walked home from a dinner party through the dark, quiet streets of my neighborhood. My family was far up ahead and I went forth slowly, noticing the way the naked poppies swayed in the shadows and watching for cracks in the sidewalk. Suddenly I looked up to see a tree, its trunk, branches, and leaves illuminated silver white by the moon frozen behind it in the ink sky. Immediately my mind flipped, like a channel changing, to a holiday fair in the dark of a Florida winter evening when I was three years old, a fifty-foot tree decorated with tinsel and beach-ball-sized pearly globes—the first Christmas tree I had ever seen, blazing as if struck by lightning; the distant churning of the ocean; the smell of cotton candy; the heavy damp weather; the wonder of the tree and the fair competing with prickly fear on the back of my neck from the specter of the KKK, which regularly marched in bright white robes down our streets.

Can you state what it is like to lose many things? It is disorient-ing, yes? Would you say it is, not to put words in your mouth, but, would you say it is perhaps discomposing? Stinging, gloomy? Exposing?

Exposed is the only real.
This book is not about . . .
Sand castles
A pleasure boat
Masturbation
Country line dancing

(I'm trying to say something but it's hard to breathe.)

Silence, cross-examined

Maybe it is not *my* silence at all. I could blame it on the fog. The fog that in this city is so near constantly present it creates a blue-hued permission to isolate oneself, a folding into. Not a permission, maybe, but a floating command. It forms a world of its own, a cocoon. A quiet burying. *Shhhhhhhhh.*
But then I would just be weak.

A lot of kids in the eighties had broken homes—do you think you could be exaggerating your response?

Pioneering female astronomer Vera Rubin discovered that spiral galaxies—characterized by a flat, rotating disc of stars, gas, dust, and a central cluster of stars known as the bulge—are composed primarily of dark matter: matter we know is there but cannot see. Sometimes I picture Vera sitting alone in the hushed hours of night, her eye pressed up against a scope, scanning the interstellar for signs beyond luminosity. Matter is all around us, she knew. Dark matter teases and haunts us from the inside.

What is the matter with you, my mother would ask, annoyed, when I posed too many questions or spoke of something that the adults in my family all agreed—all agree—without it being expressly stated, should remain obscured.

In the vital statistics compilation of Canadian families' marital unions and unravelings that goes back to 1926, just after my ancestors docked on the western continent, there is an observable bulge in the year 1987, a point on the graph where the slowly climbing line peaks. This bulge is the single year when the most divorces occurred—96,200—the year my baby brother was born, the year my parents' marital union was fraying obediently, right on track with the demographic trend.

In the central bulge of a spiral galaxy, the stars are in orbits that are random compared to the flat plane of the galaxy. Classical bulges happen when smaller structures collide, sending the stars everywhere. It seems obvious but is easy to forget: shock disrupts the paths of stars.

What is the matter?

Even if you determine to be a traitor, at first it is difficult to speak of one's own aching when that aching belongs, too, to everyone else of the same generation. Is your pain common, or unique? This might be a question of emotional parallax. The experiences of the many have a way of depersonalizing the suffering of one.

What would Hester do?

Not what my mother is doing. She is working at an office job she likes but not really making ends meet for us. She is dating a man named Chip. Chip has his own company and a large fancy home. Chip will see her on Tuesdays and Saturdays. Chip will take her but never us to nice places to eat. Chip's wife died. Chip will take her back to our house afterward but not his. Chip will sleep over on the appointed days. Chip will go to the country club. Chip will play golf. Chip will be a racist. Chip will give my mother the extra money she needs to make ends meet.

Maybe Hester would do this.

How does one relate to the land?

Sometimes my mother and I just drive around together. We make an ersatz itinerary and we get in the car and get on those highways and just *go*. We cruise the suburban neighborhoods with their rolling seas of Spanish tiled roofs and their cafes and their gardening acts in progress. We stop in at the biggest bed-and-bath store we have ever seen just to find out what they fill the aisles with. We get iced cappuccinos. We roll the windows down or crank up the air, we slide our sunglasses on, we giggle and we declare with every action we take, Yes! This is the dream! And we wonder again how we got here, shaking our heads and sometimes actually saying out loud, How did we get here? Our favorite song, by Beck, comes on the radio and we make it loud and tip our heads back and yell-sing along. We're losers, babyyyyy, so why don't you kill us.

Map for us your heart

ISLANDS

Yerba Buena, means "good herb."

Alcatraz, known as "The Rock."

Treasure, man-made for the 1939 Golden Gate International Exhibition, which opened San Francisco to the world.

The Farallons, thirty miles west of the Golden Gate Bridge, they look misty in the impossible gold of the sunset and sound like "far-along," which means if you reach them you have gone far along enough to believe that you can get to the edge of the world.

Catalina Island, an enclave of billion-dollar ice-cream-colored homes and quaintly crusting boardwalks where one sunny afternoon, a few years from now, I and a man who furnishes me a startling canon of intimacy will have one of a series of fights that will force me to disassemble my life and then put it back together like a child's fairy castle.

San Nicolas Island, of *Island of the Blue Dolphins* fame. There, in the book, dwelled Karana, a composite of Juana Maria, the last of the Nicoleño, who was abandoned on the island after a party of otter hunters killed many of her tribe and the Spanish missionaries evacuated the rest. Rumor had it Juana Maria was trying to save her little brother, who had been left behind, when she wandered off and missed the boat.

She went after her brother.

Juana Maria survived alone on the island for eighteen years in a home she built of whale bones.

Often I feel I am gazing upon California from the vantage point of an atoll, poking up off the coast, studying her the way I see the boys in sagging pants and the university professors in pleated slacks sometimes looking my body up and down.

Do you understand? I *feel* her. While I am trying not to drown, I can smell her long, westward flank—artichoke musk, garlic skins—her almond crevices and salty bays. They puddle at my feet.

Who I am kidding?

"California is often compared to a lodestone, or a magnet, or the moon drawing the tides," wrote Dora Polk. "On occasion, California is fancifully described as an enchantress—Circe, or one of the Sirens or the Lorelei. Every utopian name imaginable has been applied at some time—Atlantis, Arcadia, Avalon, the Garden of Eden, El Dorado, the Elysian Fields, the Garden of the Golden Apples, the Happy Valley, the Isle of the Blest, the Land of Milk and Honey, the Land of Prester John, Mecca, the New Jerusalem, the Pleasure Dome of Kubla Khan, the Promised Land, the Terrestrial Paradise, and Treasure Island."

A chimera.

Listen to an hour of radio, scroll through any list of movies. Gather a pile of common dreams. California is everywhere. California is everyone's.

It has never been only mine.

PART FIVE

Allegory of a Caretaking

1.

When I fall in love with the Taylors, I am a semester away from turning eighteen. Two of my own families have already exploded. Nuclear family has not proved successful, but still I am drawn to it.

I find the Taylors through their job posting, which reads something like:

> Energetic, fun Mary Poppins-type sought for three teenage girls for after-school pickup, homework, and supervision. Excellent pay, benefits. Experience preferred. Warm, pet-free family just waiting for the perfect nanny.

At first I'm not sure about working in somebody's home. I would be seeing and touching other people's stuff, inhabiting their space, I realize, overhearing their intimate family moments. I would be a witness to the things that people don't want anyone outside a family to see, things bad enough to have to witness in one's own family.

But I need money. The Taylors sound nice enough, and nannying would fit with my class schedule.

As I walk up to their front door one Saturday in October, I begin to feel hopeful. Their North Bay town of Concord is known for being rough and hot, the sun always beating down hard on the blacktop outside graffiti-coated mini-marts. But the Taylors' subdivision is nicely shaded, with orderly homes, long driveways, and tall trees that indicate, along with the architecture, that this suburb has been successfully turning out perfectly average families for a while now.

I notice matching flowerbeds flanking the front door, protected for the mild winter already under mounds of cedar chips. The curved bay window is dressed in flowing ivory drapes. *A good family home,* I think, tiny jealousies firing like subconscious cannons.

Sharon Taylor swings open the heavy wood door just as my hand reaches for the doorbell.

Welcome! she exclaims, ushering me into a formal living room. She reaches out her tanned hand, tipped with pointy, pearlescent pink nails. I'm Sharon, and this is Michael, she says, passing me to a short, buff, goateed man wearing pleated slacks even though it is Saturday morning. They invite me to sit on the couch.

I love that you speak French, gushes Sharon during my job interview. You can help Kacee with hers … if she only studied more I think we'd see a huge improvement. A tutor is exactly what she needs!

We just want a good influence on our daughters, confides Michael, leaning forward to rest his elbows on his slack-covered knees, barely glancing down at my hastily thrown-together teenage resume. Someone to get them home, help them study, make sure they do their chores, and keep them out of trouble until we get back around six. And keep the boys away.

I can absolutely do that, I say as I nod, trying to seem mature even though I am still seventeen and this will be my first job. I have experience, though. A reel of memory intrudes—the hours and years beside my brothers with their pudgy, grasping hands, storybooks, soft cheeks needing to be wiped, before we all split away like trains to opposite stations.

Immediately I feel the desire to work for the Taylors. I want to help them, these earnest parents so concerned for their daughters' well-being. I believe I alone am meant to be their nanny. I have instant visions of a long-lasting connection: I will work for them, helping to bring up the girls while I get through college, and in the process I will become a de facto daughter, an adopted member of their family. Even after the Taylor girls are grown, I'll come back here on holidays. There will be gifts for me under the tree.

And they want me, offering me the job on the spot for more money a week than I have ever had in my bank account.

I saunter back down the pebbled walkway, rosy afterglow flushing my face. Our affair, mine and the Taylors', has begun. Like all romances, at first ours will be perfect.

2.

Every weekday morning, I wake up at dawn and get myself to college, where I've registered for all morning and midday classes. After my last one, I get into my car and drive through five freeways and three interchanges to get to Concord.

We get into a routine: I pick the girls up at their schools, get home and give them snacks, supervise them while they protest about homework and then, with some prodding, do homework, and then we have free time.

There are three of them: Kayla, tall with braces, is fifteen and a tenth-grader at the high school; delicate and reserved Kacee is thirteen and in her last year of middle school; and Kennedy is twelve, sassy, and pulsing with still-childish energy.

The girls are friendly and happy that I'm here. They want to style their own hair, have me style their hair (but not style my hair because they quickly realize the long ropes of dark curls will never look smooth and polished no matter how much sparkly gel and plastic hair clips they apply), gossip, read magazines, fight with each other, paw through my college backpack, and practice cheerleading moves. Look! they call deferentially to me, whenever they are doing something cool or silly, look!

They're sporty and athletic like many of the teenage girls I have seen in the Bay Area, which fascinates me because the girls I grew up with before we moved west were lots of things—stylish, worldly, slender—but not like this.

I worry that I stare at them too much, these native specimens to whom easy, happy, girl life seems to come so naturally, but I can't force my gaze away. I have not yet been so close, and allowed such access, to Californian girls. Their bronze, lean little muscles radiate, frosted with barely perceptible blond hairs. They wear layers of thin, colorful tank tops; sloping basketball shorts or Daisy Dukes with their tiny, sun-goldened asses and toothpick legs popping out; stacks of beaded friendship bracelets up their arms. They play volleyball and soccer. They swim competitively. They eat like weightlifters.

I'm surprised that, though the weather is warm for fall, they never want to use the pool out back. They don't seem excited about it, don't seem to even notice, but I can't stop looking out at it. Every few minutes I peek at the backyard, just checking that the big, private pool is still there, sparkly and embryonic.

One afternoon they want me to dance with them. Kacee loads a CD into their parents' prized stereo equipment in the formal living room so she can blare it louder than her cheap boombox will go. A song called "Tootsee Roll" by 69 Boyz booms out from the floor speakers.

Dad's gonna kill you, Kayla snarls to Kacee, but the music's already thumping and all three girls pull me onto their carpeted dance floor.

Come on, let's see your moves! Kennedy shouts, swishing her tiny twelve-year-old behind back and forth as she drops it to the ground. Kacee reaches her hands up over her head and then arches her back as she lowers her hands back down behind her in a backbend, then kicks her legs up and over her body in a full flip like the ones that I have seen in USA gymnastics competitions. I know I should get them moving toward their homework and chores, but I am mesmerized.

Kayla launches into some breakdancey moves. Grind it, grind it! the other two cheer, laughing hysterically as I show them what must seem like my very lame, rusty old-girl moves. Let me see your tootsie rolls. I am still seventeen, just a few years older than them, barely six months out of high school, but I feel ages beyond them, yet also somehow younger than them. Like in their sisterliness and Californianess, they know something I never will.

3.

The Taylor adults usually come home around six, arriving simultaneously in their separate cars, swinging through the garage door into the kitchen, and quizzing the girls about homework and school and friends and, always, the progress made on their long list of household chores.

One night in the late fall it is dark when the Taylors sweep in, as dark as when I wake up before dawn to make it to my early classes and be done to pick up the girls in time for their school bell.

How was the afternoon? asks Sharon, dropping her bulging suede day planner on the counter. Did they get their homework done?

We had too many chores, Kayla tosses out, before I can tell them that the girls had told me they had no homework that day.

Michael kicks the fridge door closed and cracks a beer and says to me, We really need you to get a handle on their schedules.

Yeah, pipes Kennedy.

What?

No dinner started? Sharon gasps suddenly, glaring at Kacee, who has been chopping mushrooms at a furious pace since the parents pulled in.

I'm confused. It seems like we've been busy since four—we did some French conversation; we cleaned the bathroom and folded laundry; and then there was that dance breakout session … I open my mouth to tell Sharon and Michael more about our afternoon, but they have turned their backs and are huddled now over the mail, murmuring together. The girls have united in kitchen duty, drawers are banging, a gas burner clicks. The family has folded in. I'm not needed here anymore, I realize, my day abruptly done.

I wave bye and close the front door behind me, leaving the Taylors together in their steaming-up kitchen. As I slide into my car and turn my key, a feeling falls over me. *I might have had a family like this,* I think. Not the step-family that was destined to dissolve before it even formed; not my dad's new family playing out without me; but my real family. My "family of origin," I mouth, trying out the new term I picked up at school in Sociology 101.

In an alternate life, I would be driving home now to my own parents, to a family like the Taylors.

I curve tiredly around the dark on-ramp onto the wide belt of the southbound 680. Stop it, I tell myself. Why shouldn't they have a nice family?

I pick up speed. I had a house like theirs once.

The last time I saw it was seven years ago, the white brick house with black shutters and the address, *Twenty-Four,* spelled out elegantly in cursive above the black garage door. Like Alice, I can slip back there through a secret hole, down a tunnel and into a flip-flopped land where the now transforms into the then, where the seemingly magical is still happening as ordinarily as ever.

There was a square yard in the back, with a swing set and a thick maple tree in the center. It took all day, every Sunday each fall, for our father to keep up with that tree. It shed relentlessly, red and yellow and orange and brown leaves bigger than my head, crunchy floaters that sailed down like slow-motion patches of quilt. Maybe there was an long summer one year or an early winter another, but that silent shower of fat fall leaves was as predictable as our father's hands wrapped around the rake handle. There we are: me, my brother Steven, in our mittens, scrambling around the piles as our dad formed them, belly-flopping into the leaves when he turns his head in the other direction, laughing, wiping noses on our sleeves.

They told us they were getting divorced in spring, just as the lilac tree was coming into bloom underneath their bedroom window. I sat on my parents' bed, my treasured collection of neon jelly bracelets sticking to my arm. This is the detail to which my mind affixes itself (not her crying or his crying or the strange, gelatinous quality of my own tears): That upcoming summer, after years of my pleading and cajoling, we were finally supposed to become members of the community swim club. Our parents had promised. At last, it was going to be the summer of cabana chairs and hot dogs and days splashing on pool noodles with the Haltons, my best friend Erika's family, who had been pool members for two years already.

Instead, my father moved out and our house went up for sale. *Who lives in that house now?* I wonder, the Taylors' neighborhood receding fast behind me. If I squeeze my eyes tightly, I am sure I could picture myself there still, in front of my big bedroom window, reading Judy Blume, watching for snow.

4.

Christmas is huge in the Taylor household. The girls start their lists early, and I help them. Kacee, always one to butter up her parents, works unusually hard to write her list in French. For winter break they are going to Hawaii, where they go every year to lounge on the beach and cram in as many wild water sports as they can.

Leading up to their vacation, I hear from the kids about what they'll do—snorkel, water ski, tan until they're even more golden—but I hear Sharon and Michael arguing beforehand, too.

They can't afford it, the credit cards are nearly maxed, something's got to change. I don't know why, but this knowledge makes me uncomfortable, almost queasy. I think about the $300 they pay me every week, how big of a chunk of their budget that might or might not be.

It's obvious that the Taylors aren't wealthy in the way the families who live in nearby suburbs are, in Danville, Walnut Creek, Blackhawk, near where I used to live in an even-nicer-than-the-Taylors' house, exclusive communities with gates and circular driveways that shelter the beneficiaries of Silicon Valley's crazy growth. Sharon works as a mid-level bank manager; Michael does something mysterious—I can't remember what job description I was given when they interviewed me. All I know is he wears a suit and carries a black leather briefcase and drives a Corvette. And the girls seem to have all the short shorts and basketball shorts and tankinis and hair accessories they need.

I don't want to know about financial stressors. I only want to be able to afford my own guzzling gas tank and college textbooks. I want things to be all good at the Taylor house.

But lately, more and more, I'm sensing that they're not.

The girls often whisper, crowd into the bathroom, block me out of their bedrooms. At first I figure these are normal grabs at privacy, ways to hide their obsession with boys and the cheap cosmetics they somehow emerge from the mall with.

But something more feels off.

Do you have any brothers or sisters? Kacee asks me one day while I am trying to get them to sit still and do some homework. The three have been bickering all afternoon and I'm panicked about the lengthy chore list.

I have two siblings, like you, but they're brothers, I say, keeping it simple and not mentioning that one brother actually has a different father, that our family came apart after he was born. I also don't mention the step-family I had for two years, the one I came to California with.

Kacee glances knowingly at Kayla, who grimaces. Shut up, she orders.

Actually, I have a half-sister, Kacee says anyway, with a quick little grin. The girls are now looking at each other with narrowed blue eyes.

You're going to get it, warns Kennedy, smirking and shoving a handful of chips into her mouth.

Ho! Kayla hisses at Kacee.

What's going on here? I ask in as commanding a voice as I can muster. But my alarm seems suddenly to unite them, and they all clam up and pretend to be doing what they're supposed to, as if to say, *It's private, you can't know because you aren't one of us.*

Just before Hawaii, I am invited to a family concert at the younger kids' school. Sharon gets a head start with the girls while I tidy up the kitchen.

You'll drive with me, Michael says, coming downstairs in a fresh shirt.

Michael's black Corvette is parked inside the Taylors' three-car garage, and I open the door and curve myself into the front passenger seat. I've never been in a car like this before. He pauses before turning the key in the ignition, making this quiet moment before I feel the deep rumble of his sports car through the lower half of my body seem almost sacred. The automatic garage door is still closed, holding us inside.

Hot machine, isn't it? Michael says, leaning across the front seat to give the caramel leather that wraps the dashboard a stroke. How fast do you think it goes? he asks, looking at me.

The Corvette is tiny inside; we are only a few inches from each other. It smells faintly of cigar and cologne. In the low bucket seat I am half reclining.

I don't know? I ask, trying a smile.

You're about to find out, Michael says. He looks at me and then he puts his hand on my stockinged knee.

I should have seen it coming, is what I will think much later. Now I think, *I don't want to be alone in this car with him.*

But I am still in love with the Taylors, with being their babysitter. I'm not ready yet for it to end.

I think we should get going, I say, hoping to sound casual. Sharon and the girls will be waiting. He cocks his head and holds my gaze for a second that feels like a minute. His hand lifts off my knee.

Yeah, he says. And the engine roars.

5.

In February Sharon and Michael are invited away overnight to a wedding. They ask if I can spend the whole weekend taking care of the girls, and then they tell me to bring my boyfriend, Jim. Like we are a full-grown adult couple. Like we are married. This shocks me because I feel so young. I *am* so young. Neither Jim's parents nor even my own distracted mother allows sleepovers in their houses.

No, that's really okay, I say, almost embarrassed, to Sharon. I can just do it.

We really welcome Jim, Michael pushes, pulling a beer out of the fridge one day just after they breeze through the garage door after work. Please, we want you to feel free to bring him. Absolutely. You'll stay in our room. He winks at me.

That weekend Jim and I take the girls to a movie and out for burgers. It's fun; we are a band of young people doing just fine on our own. I make sure the girls behave, that their shorts aren't too short when we go to the mall, that between shrieking giggles they say excuse me after belching loudly and don't call each other hos or bitches in public. I feel safe in the suburbs that night with Jim and his cop career aspirations in the house.

But the following Monday afternoon when we get home after school, Kacee saunters over, holding out a pair of panties. With a hollow feeling in my stomach I realize they are my red panties, lacy ones I picked specifically for the occasion of sharing a bed all night with my boyfriend. I must have left them in Sharon and Michael's master bathroom by accident.

My parents thought this was *dis.gus.ting*, she informs me. All the girls have funny grins on their faces.

I am mortified, afraid the Taylors don't like me anymore. That they will want to be done with me. I shove the panties in my bag. That afternoon I let the girls goof off while I stare out at the empty aquamarine pool. It feels like they won something and I lost.

No one mentions it again, but I can't let go of what happened with the panties. Whereas before I felt like a grown adult, suddenly I feel like a poser. Like I've been exposed for what I am, too young, not ready, not a kid anymore but a pathetic excuse for an adult.

6.

After the panties, it feels like something has changed at the Taylors'. There are offhand comments about me not cooking dinner, for instance. I have no idea how to approach this. It's true that when they hired me there was casual mention of supervising the girls while they started dinner, and I have done this on nights when the girls are cooperative. I manage at least to help them chop and prep. But I'm secretly embarrassed because I don't really know how to cook, not real full, hot meals that can be ready and waiting, delicious, by the time the Taylor parents get home. My mom never taught me and I can't ask her now, not when most nights she is wringing her hands over late bills, sobbing into her pillow, or out on dates with Chip.

I'm spending less and less time at home. It sometimes feels impossible, college, the uneventful but steady continuation of dating Jim, the endless concrete commute, and managing life at the Taylors', where I need to belong but feel my welcome slipping.

Our mom and dad are really unhappy with you because our homework isn't organized enough, I sometimes hear from the girls. Their rules seem to be getting stricter, they're grounded for what seem to me like minor infractions, and their chore list grows longer. I can't muster the courage to ask the parents directly if they are unhappy with me. I have no idea how to ask, and I'm afraid of the answer. Are they waiting for me to hand in my resignation? Why? Am I like the string of bad governesses in *The Sound of Music* or whatever shitty nanny had come before Mary Poppins? I've thought back to the Corvette incident, the panties. I've racked my brain to think of anything I might have done really wrong. Besides not being a chef, I can't come up with much.

Things between the girls and me feel different, too. Before it seemed they were as infatuated with me as I was with them. But lately they seem bored, jaded, even irritated. Do you want to talk about what's going on? I ask Kayla gently one day when she seems particularly grumpy after school.

Kiss my ass, she shoots back.

Hey! I'm going to have to tell your parents, I stammer. All three girls laugh. You can probably kiss their asses too, Kayla calls lightly as she saunters off. I darken a million shades of red.

7.

In spring, the girls' uncle arrives. I'm not sure whether he is the brother of Michael or Sharon. I ask, but my questions are brushed aside. He's staying indefinitely, I'm told, and will keep to himself around the house.

Uncle Scott stays in his room most of the time, wandering down to the kitchen only to joke for a minute with the girls or get a snack. He's youngish looking, with dirty blond hair and a bit of a beer belly. His facial scruff is overgrown; he wears sweats and flannel shirts and bare feet. He hardly speaks to me. Though he does nothing obviously wrong, something about him feels odd.

What's his deal? I ask the girls one day while they are roller-blading around the cul-de-sac. Kayla stops and fixes her blue eyes on me. He did something, she says in a low voice. Something we are never, *ever* allowed to talk about. Sorry, you can't know.

Between work, commuting, classes, and studying, I am operating on very little sleep. Sometimes on the way to school I nearly doze off behind the wheel. I learn to roll down the windows to the ocean air and slap my face to stay awake. That, plus coffee and packs of M&M's, keeps me going.

One Friday, the week before spring break, I forget to leave campus an hour sooner than usual so I can pick the girls up for an early release day at their schools.

I realize my mistake in the student union, stuffing a falafel sandwich into my mouth as I glance at the wall clock. It's impossible, I realize. They'll be released in twenty minutes; it will probably take me that long just to get to my car in the student parking garage.

Freaking out, I remind myself that they are not babies. I know they won't wander into traffic and die without me being there on time, but I cannot keep my hysteria at bay. *You messed up, you made the biggest mistake*, I keep repeating to myself. I bang my steering wheel the whole way to Concord and yell at the windshield, over and over again, shaking my head. I feel like throwing up. *Nonononono*.

When I get there, an hour later than when I should have arrived, the uncle opens the door. He doesn't let me in; I just stand there on the front step.

I got them, he says casually. I called Sharon. She said you can just go home. She's not working the rest of the week, either, so you don't need to be here.

I return the next afternoon anyway, the usually long drive on the highways, the route past the 7-11, the weird scented candle shop, and the gas station where I buy gas with a gas card the Taylors gave me all passing by in a blur.

Sharon opens the door and holds it ajar as I stand again on the stoop. She arches her eyebrows.

I'm so sorry, *so* sorry . . . I begin. I really wish I hadn't missed the pickup.

And then something uncontrollable happens that I will never fully understand.

I'm really sorry I missed the pickup, I say to Sharon. But I was stuck at the hospital. I'm pregnant.

My words just hang in the air there between us.

Why do I say this?

Why would I say this?

It is a lie that does not even make sense. I must think, in the moment, on this afternoon on this stoop when I am seventeen trying to be all grown up, that if you are pregnant, which I am not, you are tested for it at the hospital. Do I think this entails a clutch of worried nurses and doctors hovering around you with clipboards? I have no idea that a pregnancy test from a drugstore is all it takes.

I do not know why I say this. But suddenly it is like the grenade has landed at my feet and I can either wait for implosion or pull the pin myself. Something in me makes me pull the pin.

Later, a long time later, I will make the connection, about pregnancy as an eject button, a release valve. About my mom and dad and the one sure thing I discovered, as a child, could force a family to burst open.

I will know that this moment on a suburban stoop is the one when everything really comes undone. When I finally come undone.

But that is not what I know right now, on the Taylor family's front step, starting to cry for shame, for so many reasons and none at all.

Sharon's face is fixed, her streaked blond hair tucked behind her ear. Time seems to have stopped, hovering around this thing I've just said, creating an awful space for it to breathe and expand.

Well, she says, her face still steady. That is hard. I have been there, believe me (and here she emphasizes her words, gives them a weight that somehow in the moment makes everything more confusing to me). But life is full of responsibilities, she goes on, and you did not follow through on yours. We won't be needing you as a nanny here anymore.

I nod and step backward from the big, carved door as it shuts, past the spring flowers in their beds, some already in bloom.

I won't ever see the girls again, will not say goodbye, will not be paid for my last two weeks of work, even after I return their house key to them in a white envelope in the mail and gather the courage to ask in the apologetic note for my wages.

As I walk away from the house for the last time, I realize that we are really through, the Taylors and I. We are over.

Something is wrong with me. Maybe I will never be normal.

This, too—my perfect, made-in-California family—has fallen apart.

Sequester:

To separate.

Sometimes juries are sequestered from outside influences during their deliberations.

After testifying, or failing to, a witness may feel spent.

Sometimes you don't get to where you want to go directly. Sometimes it is silence/eucalyptus fog/looping conversations in your dreams and you drift, hoping, toward belonging.

Self-questioning becomes painful.

You seem emptied

Everything now moves into an eddying of the elements, a process of connection more visceral: liquid, mineral, animal.

PART SIX

Ex Parte Examination of the Elements

Ex Parte:

A PROCEEDING BROUGHT BEFORE A COURT BY ONE PARTY ONLY, without notice to or challenge by the other side.

The truth:

Even though it feels like everyone is watching me, in fact no one is.

Water

Hot springs geyser out from the earth like a howl. Pool of green sulfuric water takes a body in whole, laps shoulders, wets heels, infiltrates all your caves. Oxidization: mineral, salt, bromide. On the east side of the Sierra, at the edge of the Great Basin Province, submerged in Grover Hot Springs State Park (an obvious mark in a clearing of pine forest and sagebrush) your loneliness finds corroboration in nature.

When the pool is viewed from some distance, rather than from directly overhead, the light that is reflected from the bottom loses certain wavelengths that are absorbed by the various color patterns on the bottom. The remaining light waves then pass back up through the water and are reflected at the surface. This reflected light is in the yellow-green wavelengths of the spectrum.

Because of the transitional topography of northern California's Sierra slope, a full range of seasons can occur at any time, from major blizzards to dry scorchers, warm clear nights to intense, blasting thunderstorms. Winds of great speeds are capable of whipping through the region causing damage during any month of the year. Pristine warm days can be followed by cold stormy nights. You like this idea of a transition zone.

Later in the bed of a cheap motel on the outskirts of Markleeville, you sniff your sulfur-softened skin. The Great Basin, you learn from your boyfriend, is where rivers do not flow to the sea. This makes you consider your own hydrographic patterns. You know of your own rivers: they must flow out somewhere.

Water

We've come to the wedding of his friends, cowboy types—there are still some of these in the Bay Area, out east, despite the creep of Silicon Valley yuppies. I fret over what to wear, deciding finally on a clingy flowered dress. Jim has a pickup truck now, and it bumps along a rutted road to the venue, a half-covered barn-like structure and an open circular field that looks like a vacated equestrian ring. We are in a canyon, Crow Canyon, bordered on all sides by rolling hills; leaning, wild-rooted oak trees; dusty creek beds; the occasional ranch. The bride, I see when I step out of the cab, is hugely pregnant, and for the rest of the wedding I fixate on this. How can these people our ages, Jim's and mine, nineteen, twenty-one, be near-parents? The whole of it—the cowboy hats and corral of trucks and homemade plates of deviled eggs fogging under Saran Wrap—makes me want to both stare and look away. The groom is in pressed black jeans and gleaming black boots. The bride's girlfriends and mother and aunts and sisters adjust her veil under the cover of the faded red barn roof (and this, despite partly wanting to run, I am envious of) just as heavy drops begin to coax the corral dirt into mud. A preacher appears and opens a book. The California air smells of hay, rose hip, Earl Grey tea. In the rain as she marries, the bride's dripping dress clings to her belly like a fresh, new skin.

Gold

Jim and I have been together almost four years. Because I haven't moved out of the suburbs into San Francisco, what I see around me of the kids who remain are pregnant twenty-year-olds, grocery checkout careers, girls with coiffed blond hair and quarter-carat diamond rings flashing proudly from their left hands (engaged) or right hands (promise ring).

A promise ring is what I have convinced myself I want. I think it will solve the stagnancy I feel with Jim. A promise ring, I understand, is a vague commitment to get married someday, a pledge of love somewhere between dating and marriage. Junior varsity commitment. Nevermind that Jim and I do not like many of the same things. That he watches Nascar while I read Nabokov. That his plans for his future, from what I can tell, involve becoming a police officer and buying a suburban tract home just like the one his parents have lived in for twenty-five years, while I fantasize traveling the world and maybe joining the Peace Corps before settling in a big city.

To ward off the insecurity of being twenty with the same steady boyfriend, of feeling stuck and small, I convince myself I want the ring. My imagination has been co-opted. The longer I spend in the suburbs dating Jim, the less I can imagine anything else.

I always spend Christmas with Jim's family, eating his mother's cinnamon buns, unwrapping Santa and reindeer paper to reveal the gifts they get for me, trying to delight everyone in his family with the gifts I find for them scouring the malls for hours. This year, against the tableau of a crackling fireplace, Jim hands me a small wrapped box and I inhale sharply. *This is it*, I think, the gold ring I know will set me more firmly on a life course, even if it's the blandest course. I pull the ribbon, peel back the St. Nick paper, and reveal a box, which, when I pry it open, hands trembling, contains not a gold band flecked with tiny diamonds or rubies revealing, in their sparkling facets, Jim's permanent allegiance, but a new Motorola pager.

Fire

Jim told me that once his family could have been caught and killed in a fire. They were vacationing near Yosemite National Park. For a week or more there had been intense thunderstorm activity because of warm, humid air from the Gulf of Mexico piping over California. During that period, according to a California Division of Forestry estimate, lightning hit the ground at least 16,701 times, torching tinder-dry trees experiencing their sixth year of drought. Jays screamed and sixty thousand acres were blackened. When it became obvious that they would need to leave the area, Jim's family hurriedly packed up the car and raced out on the highway before flames would close it down. I have the image, I don't know why, of not only cars pouring out of the valley and mountains, but trains, too, in queues, threading away from the fire on hot rails, of animals—mule deer, Sierra Nevada red fox, black bears, and bobcats—bolting. None of this should come as a surprise, even if your life is moving along its track seemingly uninterrupted. Firestorm, dust storm, flood, quake: all are at home in the state of California.

Fire

I go for the summer to live in Gold Country and intern as a reporter at a newspaper that still operates out of a small-town frontier building so that when I leave college with a degree in a year I will be employable somewhere. Gold Country: a part of the central California map that time forgot, where miners appeared 150 years ago to make their fortunes or die or both, 130 miles east of San Francisco, adjacent to Yosemite National Park. I will cover county fairs, Main Street candy shops, police logs, and fires.

Earth

In the calm before, I am sitting inside an historic Berkeley theater at midnight watching *The Rocky Horror Picture Show*. My costume of platform shoes and tight black everything makes it hard to scramble out of a place fast. The one thing I will remember about earthquakes is how you hear them before you feel them. In the epicenter, above the campy whine of *Rocky* lyrics, I sense it, far at first, then rolling toward me, loose and wild, a low rumble that grows into a living growl, a roar, a thunder in the earth.

Liquid

Aftershock, it is called. He feeds it to you from a frosted bottle. It is red, right? Flavored cinnamon, the liquor has a viscosity unlike water. Thicker, a hooded water, spiced ejaculate. It burns going down, and it goes down many times. You think you remember. Time passes more quickly when you are swimming in the cinnamon river. Also more slowly. Your limbs tingle, but this internal kinesthesia does not lead to actual movement. Your arms and legs and head are fixed in their positions, mudded. A morning rolls around, light filters dully into a room. Your body is in a semi-folded position, limbs swathed in the poisonous smell of cinnamon, but you do wake up. For the next three months the tips of your fingers and toes stay completely numb.

Your insides, which have been numb for a while now, stay that way for some time longer.

Metal

The frontier newspaper building was dark and cool inside. I was given an old-fashioned punch card that slipped into a metal box on the wall to register my work hours. The news staff included a rushed redheaded editor named Patty, two assistant editors, and four or five reporters. They were distracted, I thought, maybe because the newspaper was an afternoon publication. By midmorning, everyone had only a few hours in which to find and file their news. The day was always hanging over you.

On my first morning a grandmotherly woman named Emily handed me a camera, a heavy black and silver device with a black canvas neck strap, softened by years around the necks of small-town journalists.

We have a photographer, she said. But he can't be everywhere so you'll have to take your own pictures sometimes. Have you done that? I shook my head; I had never handled a manual camera.

When you come back in I'll process your film, Emily said, gesturing toward the darkroom.

Patty told me I would mostly be covering community events and filling in for staff on summer vacation.

There will probably be some action on the forest beat, too—summer here we have a lot of fires, she said. That gives reason to go out past our regular coverage areas, into Yosemite sometimes. Fires are the biggest news that happens out here, except for that killing business.

Killing business? I repeated.

The Sund-Pelosso murders, she said. We didn't cover it much, left that to the AP and the big-city papers.

She must have seen my face then; it must have blanched. They've got the guy now, Patty said, nodding her head reassuringly. It's done with.

Tree

Gold Country: deceptively suburban-looking ramblers dwarfed by sixty-foot-tall trees. I rented a room for the summer from a nurse. While the neighborhoods of San Francisco glowed their ice-cream-colored summer sunsets until ten p.m., out here the shadows curtained down on the nurse's cul-de-sac by late afternoon.

I drove down a mountain on the Golden Chain Highway to my summer job early each morning. Skinny pines dressed in dry needles pushed out of the sloped earth, purple in the dawn. Rusted billboards, long-shuttered family resorts, and park signs with names carved yellow in Sherwood-Forest script conjured a campy but deserted feel. Though the quiet stretch of two-lane state highway was flanked mostly by conifers, I got the feeling there were houses back there, too, hidden where I couldn't see.

Fire

Later, I typed "Yosemite killings" and waited for the slow tick of the nurse's dial-up Internet.

When a news page finally loaded, it told me that in February, a woman and two teenage girls—Carole Sund, her fifteen-year-old daughter, Juli Sund, and their travel companion, sixteen-year-old Argentinian exchange student Silvina Pelosso—had been abducted from Cedar Lodge, just outside Yosemite, where they were staying while exploring the area. The missing women touched off one of the largest manhunts in Sierra Nevada history. For weeks FBI agents, highway patrol officers, and National Park Service rangers combed the rugged area with dogs, helicopters, and equipment.

On March 19, on a logging road near the northeastern edge of the park among abandoned gold mines and dense forest, Carole and Silvina were found in the trunk of the charred remains of Carole's rented Pontiac. Both were burned beyond recognition, identifiable only through dental records. A note was sent to police with a hand-drawn map indicating the location of the third victim, Juli. The top of the note read, "We had fun with this one." Investigators went to the location depicted on the map and found the remains of Juli. Her throat had been cut.

I kept reading. Through the spring, police searched for the killer, who it seemed had disappeared into the woods. Then just days ago, right before I had arrived in Gold Country, the lead investigator on the case had made a public declaration: the killers were safely behind bars. Without identifying any suspects by name, FBI District Chief Jim Maddock acknowledged that media accounts had "identified some of the people we are looking at." Maddock then added, "I do feel we have all of the main players in jail." It seemed charges would be filed imminently.

There was a sense of relief, according to the news stories I scanned. Tourists were returning to Yosemite in droves, and residents believed it was safe to again walk in their woods.

Water

"Of the four million visitors to Yosemite [in 1998], just 15 were victims of violent crimes, a 70 percent drop from six years earlier," Joshua Hammer wrote in an article in *Outside* magazine called "The Yosemite Horror." "Homicides in the 54 national parks are rare; indeed, 64.5 million visitors thronged the parks in 1998, and remarkably, there were no murders. Until 1999, perhaps the most terrifying crime against women in the national parks occurred in May 1996, when two experienced backpackers, Julianne Williams, 24, and Lollie Winans, 26, were knifed to death at their campsite a few hundred yards off the Appalachian Trail in Virginia's Shenandoah National Park. The two women had been out for a five-day circuit hike in the park when they were attacked. The last homicide inside Yosemite's boundaries occurred in 1987, when a man pitched his wife off a precipice to collect on her insurance policy. According to a statistician at the University of Florida, the odds of being murdered in a national park in 1995 were about one in 20 million—less than the odds of drowning in one's own bathtub."

Water

I am swimming in the pool of my mother's apartment with Jim, Suzanne, who is visiting me in California, and Jim's friend Jackson. The day starts sunny but not hot. We have the pool to ourselves. The plan is to swim, get dressed up, go out clubbing in San Francisco later tonight. All Suzanne and I care about is that we're together. The balance of everything is only right when we are in the same place on the map. Being with each other in California, which over many visits the past few years she has come to love, too, is all that really matters. It has been this way ever since we met in the fall of sixth grade after I transferred to her school and we were put together for a research project on sharks. She loved sharks and I had zero interest in them, but I had a lot of interest in a black-haired, fast-talking eleven-year-old girl.

The thing about sharks is you can have no idea how close they are because they comprehend body motion and understand whether a human is facing forward or backward. With this intelligence a shark will always have the ability to sneak up behind its human prey. You can be navigating the most transparent waters, sand right there, shore close, pretty coral and rainbow fish undulating in the gentle swell, and then the shark is on top of you. Suzanne and I are talking by the side of the deep end when it comes to us, gliding across the pool from where the boys are play fighting in their bare chests, swim trunks like loose sails: someone, one of them, I want to think it is Jackson, makes a joke about the Holocaust. Suddenly the water is very cold. Suzanne and I get out quickly, leave them floating there like bloated bodies.

Air

or

Where is her father these days? Certainly California is not the other side of the galaxy. Why doesn't he come into the picture?[1]

The last time she spoke to him they sat in a car in Montreal, the spring before she moved away. She was fifteen. It was a cold spring, one of the coldest on record. They were in his black Volvo. They had not spoken in more than a year, since he had married his wife. When her father and his girlfriend first began dating, the divorce of her parents—the childhood home sold, the missed pool membership, the family rituals all evaporated—was still raw. The father moved in with the girlfriend and her five-year-old daughter. Meanwhile, the first daughter yearned for a feeling of family, of a house that was not going to slip down a wormhole. She was so very lonely. The father's girlfriend said that if she wanted to visit them, no problem, she could sleep on the five-year-old kid's bedroom floor. She never went to sleep on the floor.

The wedding was large, more than a hundred people, mostly the friends and family of her father's fiancée. She had been fourteen. She wanted to bring both her best friend, Suzanne, and a boy to the party. Her father said it was too much, that the new wife's family was paying for a lot of the wedding, that it was very expensive. Pick one, he said. But she couldn't pick. If she chose the boy, if she even had the courage to ask one, they could dance at the party, but there would be no one to talk to for all the rest of those hours and it would be awkward. If she picked her best friend, whom her family knew well, who felt right at home with them all, she would have a constant companion through the ordeal. But what about the dancing? She asked again for two guests or maybe the indulgence of three—a date

---

1   Note/question from Scott the copy editor: *This feels a little bit like it's breaking the rules of the book.*

Okay.

each for her and Suzanne. She was told no, stop making waves, this was not about her.

So she boycotted. She told them to take their fancy party and their stranger-guests and the overgrown baby sailor dress they had bought for her to wear to the synagogue and all the bad adult choices she thought everyone had been making recently and shove them. Surely, in cosmic terms this choice of hers would function as the event horizon of their relationship. She did not speak to them after that, and they did not speak to her. No appointments with an understanding family therapist were set up to process the chaos of their recent collective past, no mediations to talk through the ungraspable things—secrets and how the lives we know and inhabit can fade so suddenly like they had never existed. What settled instead was anger and silence, which she carried with her everywhere.

So then, in the Volvo with her father that cold spring day before she moved with the pasted-together step-family to California. Her father, understandably, was angry at the plan to take his children across the continent. Outside, the air was vapored ice, and inside the Volvo their breathing fogged the windows. Do you want to go? he asked her. His tone was clipped.

She remembered the first time she had heard of California, from the book in the school library in fourth grade. She remembered the feel of beach on her palm, the smell of the ocean from when they lived down south so long ago, just her and her mother and father in another dimension. She thought of no one knowing her, of starting new.

I guess, she said indifferently.

Well I'm going to fight to keep your brother, said her father, angrily, and this, finally, split a tiny fissure. In the freezing, fogged-up car her tears stung. She thought of her middle brother, the only other thread that connected both her parents to each other and to her, the four of them to one another. She thought of their baby brother, of his different father, all these entangled people, the connect-the-dot games they played with scratch-and-sniff markers stretched out on the carpet on quiet afternoons, of how impossible it was in real life to connect the dots, scattered stars across space.

Please don't fight it, she begged. We need to stay together. And this at least, it seemed, he granted her.

Stone

Here I keep coming back to that Junípero Serra statue. I can never recall where it is in the city when I want to find it, but when I am not looking it is everywhere, in the pink shadows of Golden Gate Park, along the sands of Ocean Beach, on the footpaths of my university where I walk with my eyes on asphalt: the father of the ruthlessly colonizing California missions in his concrete robe, one of a long caravan of men inviting themselves in to rape the western frontier.[2]

2   I wasn't going to put this in here, but something made me think of it. Just before I leave for Gold Country, I am working at the college newspaper, where I scraped together the courage to run against two other students for Editor in Chief and got the job. Once a week we stay late, pasting up each page, proofing, correcting. I drive the pages down to the printer just before midnight. One night a guy on the staff offers to come with me to the printer if I drop him off at home afterward. I pull in front of his apartment building on a steep San Francisco street, the sky like a black pudding inches above us. Why don't you come up for a quick drink, the guy asks me, jutting his thumb toward the window. No it's okay, I answer lightly, believing I am actually being asked. Just one, he says. Aww, thanks, but I need to get home, I say, putting my hand on the gear shift. Come on, just for a bit, he presses, the voice too serious now for the request. No thank you, I say, as everything closes in, the pudding sky, my chest. Come up, he snarls. Next time, I force myself to promise him, as casually as I can lie. He gets out.

Water

My father had a California dream before any of us. When he was seventeen he gathered his high school buddies, bought an old VW van, and headed west on a wild trip across Canada and down the West Coast. My mother, fifteen and already his girlfriend, was left behind for the summer. Picture: early seventies, band of boys, long hair, bell-bottom jeans, Chuck Taylors, threadbare white T-shirts hugging lanky frames, tents they could only half operate, seizing their freedom. My grandmother probably handed him a canister of homemade poppy-seed cookies as he left, trailing down the driveway in her flowered housedress pleading, Take care of yourself! to their back bumper.

Who knows what happened on the way out west. Girls, diners, national parks, and dutiful postcards. Young lungs filled, between Kent puffs, with exhilaration. The important part is what happened in the Golden State. They took turns driving the van. One evening after crossing the border from Oregon and meandering south along the coast, whoever was at the wheel veered west, off Highway 1, their goal to get to the fabled California beach as soon as possible. Fog had set in. Probably some of them were asleep or stoned. The driver followed his instincts, the smell of salt, the *shhhhhhhh* of surf. But the epic California fog, like rolling secrets, like vaporized pearls, encased the VW and before they knew it they heard, they *felt*, sloshing all around them. As they came to their senses they sensed themselves inside a swell. Whoa, man, whoa! The driver crawled to a stop. They popped open the side door, looked down and saw themselves, van and all, embedded already in the Pacific. Sitting in the ocean, waves lapping mesmerizingly around them, marine life starting to seep through their

Chucks. California, with her mist and her myths, her tiding amniotic, had called them like a siren, so sweetly they washed right into her.

Plasma

California is a dream. My father knew it. Before our family came into being he went there in a fabulous van on a timeless journey fueled by boyhood myths. It loomed over us most of my childhood, unspoken but crackling with magnetic pull, a rich state of dark matter, the heart of promise. Mysterious but everything. The distant frontier, the farthest type of life from ours, the place the Beach Boys sang about from the grooves of spinning 45s, connected to us by a current of energy and a hazy wish. A centrifuge from which everything spun. The thing we could achieve separated but never together. It spoke to me my whole girlhood, one Eden spun out from another.

California is a fable. A fantasy. A fiction.

A metamorphosis.

Crystal

Jim and I traveled once underground to a place not far from the Gold Country town where I spent a summer. In his truck after a long quiet drive we pulled into the parking lot of the Mercer Caverns and followed a guide down a narrow set of rock stairs. With each step the California sky above us shrunk, a blue hole closing, until we were entirely absorbed by the dark, thin air inside the earth. The stairs circled into a wide-open room and, side by side but not holding hands, we stood silent as the glow of lanterns illuminated a castle.

Fur

For the Gold Country newspaper, I go to the county fair. I'm asked to find any story I want among the whirling rides and fried cotton candy. In a covered ring I come across a red-haired boy about ten bent over a young cow, sweeping a brush down the animal's hide. I ask if I can interview him and the boy says yes, flashing me a shy smile.

He's in 4-H, of course, and has raised the cow since birth. I know nothing about livestock and will not remember the breed, but I'm stunned at the softness of its fur up close. From a distance cows appear untextured. In actuality their fur is dense, a shag rug rising and falling with beast breath and blood.

You must be proud, I say to the boy. What will you do after the contest?

We'll sell her for slaughter, he says. I want to believe my eyes when I think I see his own quiver.

Tree

In spite of its beauty, I found Gold Country hard to navigate. There were not many landmarks, nor many buildings once you got away from a town's pioneer-themed central square. Nature overtook civilization and to me it all looked identical: sun-dappled country roads one after another; fields of hay bales and chewing cows; parched barns; curtains that rippled above windowsills; carpets of wildflowers.

While driving to or from my assignments, which were mostly some distance off—rural homesteads, state parks, and neighboring towns with names like Angel's Camp and Confidence and Twain Harte, which hosted the conjoined spirits of literary myth-makers—I had to look frantically for road names every time I came to an intersection. I was always disoriented, armed only with a basic cell phone that didn't work outside town. I learned that street signs are not a given in the country and the more you need one, the less likely it is to be there. One empty rural road forks to others. A *Thomas Guide* became my talisman: I figured out how to look up roads that began with numbers, ponds with no names, clapboard houses planted at the ends of posted no-trespassing lanes. I held the spiral book of county map pieces on my lap as I pointed myself from one story to the next along still and softly chirping roadsides, checking and re-checking the map key and my odometer for clues of distance, the faint thumping of my heart sounding like a roar in my ears. The possibility of getting lost was real and hung over me every day, and it made each assignment seem mildly threatening.

For the first time in my life, it felt like no one was keeping track of me. There was someone waiting for my story assignments to be filed by noon or one p.m., yes, and my clumsily snapped images, but after that the editors turned their attention to the needs of newsprint and ink and would not think of me until I came into the building again the next morning. If I slid down a rocky embankment, no one would know. No one would know if I didn't come home at night (the nurse I lived with was gone at the hospital for days at a time). Jim was often not around when I called and had not come to visit any weekend since I had moved to Gold Country. I tried to allow myself to submerge into this sense of isolation, to submit to a dominating loneliness. Hadn't I wanted to no longer feel like I was being watched?

One day after my work shift I decided to drive to Yosemite and hike. I would weave my way into the forest, leave my car somewhere and forge into the remoteness on foot to confront it because that seemed to be the thing to do out here. I would learn to love being alone in this wilderness, I thought, navigating my car east on Highway 120. I would coerce myself into a free spirit or terrorize myself trying. "Bohemia has never been located geographically," Bret Harte wrote in 1860, "but any clear day when the sun is going down … you shall see its pleasant valleys and cloud-capped hills glittering in the West."

But by the time I got to Big Oak Flat, barely the true mouth of wildness, I was clammy. However it is possible to feel at once that no one is watching you and yet someone is—I found that possibility. Veering to the jagged right edge of asphalt, I pulled off the road, swung into the arc of a U-turn, and sped away from my own foreboding and the forest's infinite unseen.

Rock

The weeks roll on. My summer is a stack of paper news stories. In the nurse's wood-paneled rambler, I reread them to remember what I've done, where I have been.

On June 13, 1999, an intermediate-sized rock fall of about 279 cubic yards (660 tons) forces me all the way into Yosemite. The rock fall has killed one climber and injured two others who were climbing along a route beginning near the top of the eastern talus cone at Curry Village, immediately below the "release area." Knowing nothing about rock, I am to write a story, conducting interviews about the impact on tourism and getting "local color." In speaking with park geologists I learn the travel of rocks along the talus and airborne splatter of rock was very similar to a previous "release event" on November 16, 1998. The arch-like rock mass involved in this rockslide was composed of granodiorite and tonalite rocks from a unit included in the Sentinel Granodiorite. A trigger for that event cannot be determined, though daily temperatures did fall below freezing for eleven of twelve days before failure.

ABSTRACT: Curry Village was established in 1899 and eventually extended upslope onto two major talus (debris) cones that are themselves the result of prehistoric rock falls. Part of the charm of Curry Village is the presence of the cabins amongst huge boulders. The currently active release area is above the eastern part of a large composite talus cone behind Curry Village. The lower portion of this cone is an area referred to as the Terrace and contains tent cabins used for seasonal housing for employees.

On June 23, when I am sent by the newspaper back into the park to report subsequent crumbling stemming from hairline cracks developing after the recent fatal slide, some of the airborne splatter pieces, approximately the size of footballs, reach the wood-platformed tent cabins and, falling at steep angles, pierce the canvas roofs of tents 28 and 36, break beams, and fall to the floor. The propagation of cracks is accompanied by occasional audible rock popping.

"If you grow up in California, Yosemite is holy," writes author Dennis McDougal in his book *The Yosemite Murders*. The climber's death within these boundaries of national park splendor and legend sent those in the region back into a state of being on edge.

Water

It seems stupid, but I am afraid to use the nurse's hot tub at the house where I'm staying. It is set out on her back patio, which because of the slope of her mountainside lot is raised two stories off the ground, surrounded by the spikey trunks of tall pines. I am afraid to place my body outside, alone, exposed. I am afraid of not being able to reach the door to the house fast enough if I should need to. Of being a beacon of soft flesh under a night of shadowed mountain sky. Of slipping in wet feet should I need to run across the cedar patio. Of, of, of.

Grass

Joie Ruth Armstrong, twenty-six, is a friendly, strawberry-blond naturalist from Orlando who works at the nearby Yosemite Institute. Armstrong is as at home in the backcountry as I am not, leading hikes and teaching visitors, many of them children, about the history of Yosemite's indigenous plants, animals, and geology. Joie lives with her boyfriend, Michael, another naturalist, in a nearby pine cabin they call The Green House, a rustic building where they chop wood to stay warm on crisp nights and haul water up from the creek to boil tea and admire the beauty of the glen outside that was cleared ages ago by yet another fire. Beauty birthed from annihilation.

I don't meet Joie, but if I did I feel we could be friends. She is the kind of friend I desperately need in my currently friendless-in-Gold-Country state, a woman five years older than me who is not terrified by independence but energized by it. Someone who has figured out how to be at ease, who talks to everyone and has many friends. Someone who writes in a letter to a girlfriend back home in Florida: "I love Michael with my soul and every last cell in my body. I love the big meadow with all its daisies and incredible history."

I do not meet Joie. On July 21, she packs her car for a trip to Sausalito. With Michael gone, and despite the reported news that suspects were in custody, she had told friends she was worried about a possible murderer on the loose after the killings of Carole, Juli, and Silvina. At dusk, just before she leaves her cabin for her trip, a car pulls up the dirt road. The young man inside the car confronts Joie, forces himself inside the cabin with a gun, gags her, binds her hands and feet, drags her outside, shoves her into his car and drives up the road.

Joie attempts to escape, jumping from the moving vehicle and running 150 yards before the man catches her, cuts her throat, decapitates her, and leaves her body in the forest not far from her beloved Green House at the edge of a golden meadow.

Three days after her murder, Joie's killer is caught. Once he is in custody, it immediately comes to light that he also killed the mother and two teenage girl tourists that winter. Law enforcement officials are forced to admit to the general public that since June 10, for the past six weeks at the height of the summer tourist season, the serial killer was on the loose in and around Yosemite hunting women while they had mistakenly assured terrified locals and wary travelers that the culprit in Carole, Juli, and Silvina's killings was already in jail. "We have all of the main players in jail, but we are in no rush to charge them," FBI chief James Maddock had told the newspapers in June.

Furthermore, the killer had actually been questioned by FBI agents in February, days after the three tourists were reported missing but before their bodies had been found. Finding nothing suspicious enough about him, police had let the killer go.

Necessary concocted interrogation with real-life news responses

Why did you tell the media that there was no fear of a killer on the loose, when in fact there was?

"I'm confident we've done everything that could be reasonably done."

Why didn't your department, during its investigation that winter and spring, contact transportation outlets in the area, including the cab driver who said she picked up a man matching the killer's description from Sierra Village near where Carole and Silvina's bodies were later found and gave him a $125 cab ride back to Yosemite Valley?

"These are not for the most part Perry Mason moments, where you interview somebody and they immediately confess. They aren't solved in 30 minutes,[3] like on television."

How do you explain the fact that you could have prevented the murder of another woman in Yosemite if your team had done its job?

"I've struggled with that issue for the last 24[4] hours and continue to do so."

Was Joie's killing a preventable tragedy?

"It was a tragedy, but was it a tragedy caused by not doing what should have been done? I don't think so."

---

3   Note/question from Scott the copy editor: *I would spell this out, unless it is from a transcript of some kind, in which case, can you provide that info?*
      I will not.

4   Note/question from Scott the copy editor: *Ditto.*
      Ditto.

What do you think the repercussions should be when the FBI has a killer in their hands, then lets him go, and the killer kills again?

"From the standpoint of the FBI's Washington management, it's always hindsight and Monday morning quarterbacking."

Pulp

I have a dream I am inside the pages of a *Thomas Guide* at the center of a two-dimensional mint green topography, cartographic elevations undulating in black wavy lines, county divisions and paper borders cordoning off a knoll upon which sits a steaming hot tub; a quaint green cabin represented as a pile of modest lines in the left-hand corner; all the bodies of water—hairline streams, pebble-shaped lakes, rivers, forks, deltas, creeks, narrows—inked red, for blood.

Fur

A few nights before I leave Gold Country I am alone in the nurse's kitchen. I look out the sliding patio doors and see eight glowing points of light. As my eyes try to adjust to the dark behind the points, a low growl crawls toward me. Two paws with sharp claws levitate off the ground, rise up and slam forward into the door, then two more and two again, allowing me to see in an instant the forms of four large raccoons, their thick underbodies streaked flaxen, amber, burnt bronze, banging on the glass, roaring to be let in.

Rock

One day many years after, I have a memory of climbing the rocky line of a mountain in Yosemite with Jim, of my legs trembling uncontrollably on a rough-hewn staircase because my fear of heights would not let me take another stony step forward. What route did we take? I google "Yosemite hikes." Clear in my mind is a hot, rough ascent, a backed-up line of hikers ahead of me, cable handrails on either side, my hands shaking on the cables, a definitive point at which, after hours of pushing myself through fear to progress, I said, No, and would not move any farther and turned around. For the lay hiker there are only a couple of choices in Yosemite that seem familiar to my memory. A modest day hike to Vernal Falls involves an often-wet stone staircase. The images from the internet, with other tourists grinning in the sun from their various moments of conquest, look like somewhere I might have been. Like somewhere I could feel if I close my eyes. But, though there are granite stairs wet with waterfall spray and some twisting, turning railings to grab on one's crooked climb, there is no straightforward stepped path with cable rails of the kind my mind recalls. There is such a path, steep and exposed, on another hike: the eight-mile ascent to Half Dome. From my google search returns, the images of this trail loose a tremble in my fingers so that even typing becomes difficult. I can feel the urge of Jim's body behind me, the safe but never-changing. To go forward, or not. C'MON, GIRL. But we would not have hiked sixteen miles in a day, nor planned to scale a steep four hundred-foot final vertical stretch like the one Half Dome's summiting requires. Is it a false memory, this believed communion with rock and steel and the sheer cliff of my worst fears, on the edge of a Pleistocene formation whose striking profile represents the majesty and mythos of California herself? Millennia can disappear considering California and how one lone body figures in her long scope. How was I there when I wasn't? I read on about the formation of the valley, the Sierra block, the domes, numerous fracture joint planes. Uplift, erosion, exfoliation, the pattern of glaciation and thaw, of constantly coming into a state of being.

National park parallax

"Sacred ... ethereal ... eternal. Cathedral," writes author Dennis McDougal, who started out as a California newspaper reporter just like me.

"Yosemite renews."

State their names for the record

Carole.
Juli.
Silvina.
Joie.

PART SEVEN

In Which New Breaks Away from Old

Am I an island?

When I return to San Francisco for my last year of college, Gold Country feels like a complicated dream that had placed me several *Thomas Guide* pages from horror but which helped to blow out some of the fog from my mind. I am still afraid of trying to make connections with new people, and I talk very little with my family about my life or what I am thinking about my future.

But I am thinking about it, and I find the idea of outmaneuvering silence hopeful. In Gold Country I had quietly moved my body all over a landscape like a chess board, while a killer had quietly moved his body across the very same scene. But I had also interviewed everyday people, teenagers with their high school diplomas fresh in hand, farmers eyeing the creep of Bay Area subdivisions, a hairdresser who dreamed of saving enough so she could afford a trip to Hawaii. As a journalist, I will be able to facilitate other people telling their stories, to exercise their own voices. Maybe if I can help other people speak, I can become brave enough to speak in my own life. I will have to forge a new way of being in my mind and in my body without concern for who is watching me, or not watching. This scares me. I doubt that I deserve this unapologetic pleasure.

California here I come

A golden, transcontinental thread connects Puritanism and the California myth, the latter a reflection of the prior's themes of renunciation and gratification, argues Neil Smelser, a UC Berkeley sociologist:

"A myth has a structure that is ambivalent in at least two senses: it contains a wish and its appropriate negation, and it permits an ambivalent orientation to each of its parts on the part of the hearer."

The psychological tensions of the Puritans were rooted in the guiding belief that everyone's destiny was predetermined by God. "Max Weber regarded this doctrine as one of extreme inhumanity which must above all have had one consequence for its adherents: a feeling of unprecedented inner loneliness of the single individual."

To cope, adherents decided to act in the world in a way that could surface the surest signs of salvation—this took the form of "sober self-denial and systemic self-control," of valuing labor and frugality above all else. They felt that if they found success while employing such self-control surely it was a sign of God's blessing.

The irony is that this ascetic discipline, in matters of farm, flesh, and feeling, led to capital reward, to pride, and to a different but equally entrenched angst for the Puritans: guilt.

Like a fun house mirror, then, is the California myth: gold and other wealth there for the taking. "The California myth is the negation of Calvin … for it renounces work and discipline and revels in worldly pleasures," writes Smelser. The whole family of California myths—the manifest destiny of James Polk, John Muir's worship of nature, the pretend world of Hollywood and the magic of being "discovered" and put on the big screen—imbues the land and air itself. Embedded in these riches, too, is the risk of retribution: the Donner Party deaths; the earthquakes; all our failures to fully capitalize, personally and economically, on the opportunities afforded by California, and the schadenfreude of everyone else watching you miss.

California, then, is a kind of religion. "Freedom from guilt. Freedom from obligations. The purifying powers of change"—these are the tenets of the religion of California, writes another California sociologist, Mark Juergensmeyer.

This idea comes to life in the Sophie B. Hawkins video for the song "California Here I Come," in which a sexy, East-Coast-freed Sophie speeds into sun-drenched California in a convertible and dives into sparkling swimming pools while a preacher clad in black holding a staff follows her disapprovingly around the desert.

Sophie doesn't care about the rules she's breaking. "I started becoming less and less confident when it was really time for me to be more extroverted," the inimitable Sophie says in her documentary *The Cream Will Rise.*

In other words, as Sophie almost sings in a more well-known song, free your mind and you won't feel ashamed.

I would rather be a performer than an imposter

I begin to work part time at a weekly independent newspaper in San Francisco that covers politics and the alternative arts scene. Sometimes, often, while sitting on the commuter train or lying in bed, I fantasize myself living as if in a film. In my documentary life I am in San Francisco, like in real life, but it is different. We see "me" from the outside, and there is a sense that whatever happens to me will happen because of what I choose to do but is also pre-determined. It is poignant that in my imagined life I am being captured by the camera, because in my real life I am experimenting with being a film critic. The newspaper sends me to watch indie films in aging classic theaters where I sit alone in the dark, my sweaty thighs cooling quickly on velvet seats, open to the screen. The smell in these theaters is mauve dust and Victorian lace and metal film canisters, sailors' forty-eight-hour leave and mink and loneliness. My pen lights up—it was given to me by Jim, from whom I am growing more distant, who hates subtitles and the sabulosity of the city and never wants to see these films with me, who is good but flat, who is not a Hollywood story anymore but a technical manual. The fantasized audience watches me.

What's the problem now?

Jim and I did watch some movies together, mostly the action stories he preferred. But once I made him watch *Schindler's List.*

The scene that haunted me the most was that of the young girl in the rose-red coat wandering around the black, gray, and dirty-white ghetto. The richness of the color in the bleakest of backdrops, life at the knife edge of death. As I watched with tears falling down my face I wondered who we had left in our wake, my family who was questioned and then granted passage across borders.

It can break you open, to detach from everything you come from. To be cut or cut yourself loose. It is the heart of loneliness inherited; an emptiness. The impediment to assimilation even as our hunger for it devours us.

I think after the movie Jim understood this a bit more—one thing I could leave him with.

Some of them wrote testaments

Some of our people were from Smolensk, which lay outside the Pale of Settlement and where the Jewish population rose dangerously to 10 percent in the years leading up to pogroms and violence. For a while it seemed they could live, and then the hoax was over.

She might have known the boy, the soldier, while the family lived still in Russia. A boy maybe from her hometown. Or, no, perhaps a man, not a boy, whom she really did meet for the first time on the ship. Did they lock eyes in the bread shop of a small village in the western palm of the Russian empire as fires and smoke rolled silently toward them? Or did he press hard up against her, she arched in receipt, gasping down the rancid hot choke of terrorized bodies packed into a hull and a thin cold current of Atlantic air spraying through the rusted porthole in relief, like a holy blessing?

Did it matter, by the time my great-great-aunt invited him to invade her, that he was a soldier? We must assume, in any case, that he was Jewish, or he would not have found himself an emigrant to the other side of the world, aching to slough off violence, daring to hope for reinvention.

In any case, they both would have been primed for a becoming.

How does one split oneself off?

Jewish soldiers were the first among Jews of Eastern Europe to develop dual identities. Separated from their families and communities, lower ranks of Jews, especially those who served beyond the Pale, were neither fully observant nor fully assimilated into the Russian Orthodox, predominantly peasant-origin milieu. Most Jewish soldiers kept together, helping one another preserve traces of communal identity. In 1891, some twenty thousand Jews—mostly reserve soldiers and their families—were banished from Moscow. By the 1890s—attacked for being less than Russian patriots, cunning draft dodgers, and useless soldiers unfit for combat—Jews in the army found themselves segregated. They had one foot in each world, indefinitely in a kind of paralyzed, embedded exile.

My great-great-aunt, like Chava, daughter of Tevye,[1] would have spent her young years divided in a different way: inside her parents' home, writing letters, stirring soup, milking cows, laundering beds, caring for younger siblings, and looking out the wooden shutters toward the forest and whatever could be beyond. When he came, he was worth the loss of everything that was left behind.

What, I wondered, would love like that feel like?

....

1   Question from Scott the copy editor: *Will readers know this reference?*
I just want to be visible.

Is this the denouement?

FADE IN:

EXT. TWO SUBURBAN HOUSES – NIGHT

As the winter sun fades behind the strip malls, lights flip on inside the tract houses of California's quintessential bedroom community, San Ramon.

INT. SUBURBAN HOUSES – BEDROOMS – NIGHT

Each on their telephones inside their bedrooms, the young man and young woman hold their breaths as a difficult conversation ensues.

NATALIE, in her last year of college, tired of the claustrophobic limitations of the suburbs and her boyfriend of five years but afraid to cut herself loose into the unknown—unable to see the life ahead—cradles the phone like a beige bulwark.

> NATALIE
>
> I'm graduating soon. I want us to talk about what's going to happen.

JIM, two years older than Natalie but still inching along in community college, cocks his ear to the receiver and casually lifts his foot, clad in a white and neon green Nike sneaker, up onto his bedpost.

> JIM
>
> Like what?

NATALIE

(Twirls phone cord around finger and
puts a coil of her hair in her mouth)

I'm probably going to need to get a reporter job wherever I can find one. That might mean moving to another part of California. They have schools everywhere, so maybe you could transfer or . . .

JIM

Yeah . . .

NATALIE

It might be hard but what I am saying I guess is that there is a way for us to stay together and I am willing to put in, like, 110 percent. How much can you put in?

JIM

(After a long silent pause, over phone)

Zero, I guess.

NATALIE

Zero?

JIM

Yeah.

NATALIE

I guess this is decided then.

In Natalie's bedroom the phone CLICKS into its base and a DIAL TONE SOUNDS.

DISSOLVE TO:

EXT. SUBURBAN STREET

The moon slides up over lawns.

I meet a girl named Cindi

I meet a girl named Cindi who starts inviting me out to go dancing with her. The first night, I pick her up from her apartment and she flops down into my passenger seat. She looks over my outfit—boot-cut jeans, fitted black top, dark curly hair long and loose down my back—and nods in approval.

What's up girl? Are you ready to get fucking crazy? she asks, stuffing a cotton bag under the seat.

Change of clothes, toothbrush, she explains.

I raise my eyebrows: we're supposed to be coming back to her place tonight, but I don't say anything.

I'm taking you to Rick's. I hope you have your drinking bra on. Turn right here, Cindi jabs her thumb toward the window.

I force a grin. What exactly does she mean by fucking crazy? I wonder, kicking up a cloud of dry leaves as I peel out of the apartment's parking lot.

Not that I'm worried about impressing her. Cindi isn't cool in the way truly cool girls are; she isn't untouchable. We met last spring working at a coffee shop; Cindi still works there and doesn't have any career ambitions beyond pulling espresso shots. She doesn't intimidate me, I decide, taking in her apple-scented hair and lip shine.

Inside the club there's a long bar along the side and a dance floor at the back, where techno-pop music is playing. Cindi goes straight for the bar and orders for both of us. The drink she passes me is laced with a limey syrup and strong. Cheers! she says, clinking hers to mine and then gulping. We edge into a little bar table and survey the scene, which is mostly guys in their twenties parked blankly with their beers, looking punky in their saggy jeans and white collared shirts. At the back some girls in tight skirts grind with each other on the uneven floor tiles; one in a lacy bustier is climbing into a wire cage at the top of a few steps. What a skank, Cindi tells me, nodding at the cage girl, who has invited her friend in with her. The two are now gyrating against each other behind the bars, and a couple of the guys up front have noticed and start moving toward the back.

Come on, Cindi yanks my sleeve and we go to the bar.

What's next, ladies? the bartender asks us. He's wiry, with a blue bandana hanging out of his jeans pocket.

What's your name? she demands.

Jack, he answers. He's wiping down the bar with a towel, slowly.

Is that your real name, or the bar name you give all the women who ask? Cindi cracks her gum. I wonder where she put it while she downed her lime drink.

Jack stops wiping and looks up. Real name, he says, as if he has a million times before. The bored eyes are pale, like river ice. He's beautiful.

What do you think would be good for me? Cindi asks this while leaning forward, so that her stretchy tube top gapes, revealing an almost imperceptible amount of cleavage.

Bartender Jack looks at her, then me, then back at Cindi. Beer for you, he says to her, and something fruity for you, flicking the ice eyes back to rest on me. Huh, Cindi says, leaning back onto the barstool, Yeah, whatever.

The night fast-forwards fuzzily. At some point, we end up on the dance floor, which has gotten crowded, tripping over each other and shouting into the ears of a couple of guys who are trying, I think, to pick us up. Finally, when the metal cage empties out, Cindi grabs my hand and drags me up the three metal steps and into it. She clangs the door shut and begins to dance with her arms in the air. I close my eyes, tip my head back, and start to sway.

By one a.m. I realize Cindi is way more drunk than I am. Her voice has gone to a high-pitched shriek and she's wobbly. I leave her near the front of the club to find some water at the other end of the long bar. When I come back, Cindi is standing on top of a barstool with one black spiked boot on the bar. A middle-aged guy with a gold watch is holding her hands and balancing her weight while she lifts her other foot up onto the bar. I think my jaw drops. Once up on the bar, Cindi swigs the last of her drink and then, faster than I really understand what is happening, wriggles out of her tube top and flings it out to the gathering crowd.

She's now up on the bar in her jeans and a transparent black bra, grinding her hips and laughing.

I'm frozen to the grungy floor, but my mind is moving fast, fumbling through my options. Should I pull her down? I can imagine how much all these men would love to "help" Cindi out right now. I am thinking there's no way I am going to convince her to leave when Bartender Jack, who's come down from the other end of the bar and noticed a tall blond girl with AA tits and no shirt stomping his work surface, leans toward me. You gonna get your friend off my bar? he says, low, into my ear. I sway a little myself. I don't know if it's the alcohol or the problem of my naked acquaintance/friend on the bar or Bartender Jack's mouth this close to mine.

Just then, Cindi seems to crumple. She reaches down for the bar top with her hands but one slips off. Two of the guys catch her and lift her down. She mumbles something in my direction, laughs, then passes out. Get her some air, I hear someone say. And then we are outside.

We stay out here, Cindi lying on the sidewalk, me sitting on the curb. She's still in just her bra, so I drape my sweater over her. The crowd has floated back inside after someone determines Cindi is fine, just really drunk. After a while she wakes up. We hobble to my car, and I drive us home.

Some things are hard to qualify

I'm in love with my editor at the newspaper. Fallen into obsession, or at least a prolonged state of wanting. I sit at my desk outside his office crossing and uncrossing my legs, bouncing my knee, typing my film reviews into the computer while one eye slides to the right every thirty seconds to look for his thick head of black hair poking out of the doorway.

I think about him at night until I can fall asleep and then I dream about him. Zev. He is ten years older than I am. He lives with his parents in his house on a hill in San Francisco. He drives a Volkswagen. He loves baseball. Sometimes I need to go into his tiny office, something that causes me to sweat and fantasize incessantly. He always invites me to sit. He gives me plum reporting assignments when I should be doing calendar entries. He praises my work. After six months he offers me a full-time job. You have to come work for me, he says, leaning over his desk. Those dark eyebrows. I fight the urge to drop out of college the next day.

For the first half of the year, Zev is single. His girlfriend has broken up with him. This is my window: I could ask to buy him a drink after work under the auspices of getting some mentorly advice. I could ask for career guidance. I could—

Instead I stay quiet.

How should I categorize our balance of power?

I met you in Hunters Point when I was a student at San Francisco State, where the nation's first ethnic studies department was birthed out of anger and unrest. I was the only white girl walking through the neighborhood on my way into the building where you supervised the innards of an independent newspaper in its twilight, where thirty-two years before, not far away, a white police officer killed an unarmed black boy, sparking a riot that surged through the city like a seiche; it was just afterward across the bay that the Black Panthers came up. You sent me to the Fillmore, where I found my voice enough to talk to the surviving mothers and fathers of a movement, the barber-shop owners, the jazz entrepreneurs, the grandmothers, the youth activists working with the kids. To hear their voices and write down the important things they had to say. I brought back to you the stories I could find of the old San Francisco and the new, your news assistant, your time traveler, your willing servant, and I lay those stories, breathless, at your ironically adorable Vans-clad feet.

This went on until it was time for me to graduate from college and go away and start my life.

Draw a map of your heart

In my movie life you and I are together. We are both characters for the screen, people who wander from the Sunset District to the mouth of the bay, who are wide open and uncluttered and as empty as the freshly unloaded vessels sitting in the port's dark waters. Via telescoping cameras I am seen pushing my fingers through your black hair. In the climactic scene we are shirtless and facing each other (close-up, please) and the space between the parts of our skin that are most nearly touching is only the width of two vintage copper pennies and when we open our mouths to breathe in the fog that space disappears. Your lips pull my nipple in softly, but what comes next is an eruption.

What do I keep on replay?

In another scene I am Mary Ann from *Tales of the City* except it's not the 70s it's 2000 and everyone is in business suits with big shoulders and I live in Coit Tower, the one they erected at the top of Telegraph Hill in 1933 and named after Lillie Hitchcock Coit, the wealthy eccentric and patron of the city's firefighters. Coit Tower is shaped like a cock, the head of which I live inside. Every day I/Mary Ann let down my fire-engine hair and you climb up it, your black hair rustling in the breeze off the San Francisco Bay, and you come inside the open window at the top of the tower and we sit at a table for two and have espresso and share the *New York Times*.

Why can't I just confess my desire for him?

Weak-kneed, I do ask myself this.

"Every woman has known the torment of getting up to speak," wrote Hélène Cixous. "Her heart racing, at times entirely lost for words, ground and language slipping away—that's how daring a feat, how great a transgression it is for a woman to speak—even just open her mouth—in public."

I could not confess it to him. But I could confess it to myself, and silently I sunk into it, absorbing the desire, massaging it, taking it into my cavities and factions for storage, for use afterward. This desire, in waves. It would come in handy.

How can I explain this better?

I'd be speechless before you even now, and that is something I can never ever change.

Remember what knowledge is needed

It's Thanksgiving. We're Canadian, so turkey day is nothing big for us, and my mother plans to go with her boyfriend to his country club. Normally I would be at Jim's, helping his mother arrange little black-hatted Pilgrim placeholders along the freshly polished dining table. Instead, I accept Cindi's invitation to her place.

When I walk into the tiny studio, steam is wafting into every corner.

I started dessert already, since the oven won't fit more than the turkey. Hope you like apple pie, Cindi tells me, wiping a knife off on the apron she is wearing.

And because I know your fancy ass doesn't like beer, she goes on, I bought you a bottle of wine.

She twists off the cap and pours me a glass, smiling at herself. I take it, distracted—my brain is still stuck on the fact that Cindi is dressed in an apron, and not a racy French maid apron you'd find in a costume shop but the real kitchen kind, with little cornucopia fruit baskets all over it. With her blond hair in a loose bun and her glasses on, which I've never seen, she looks shockingly domestic.

The apartment is tiny, even for a studio. Cindi's bed is almost in the kitchen; you can sit on the edge of the bed and grab a drink from the fridge. On the kitchen counter, a small raw turkey sits in a roasting pan, and Cindi is working it over with a basting stick. Ingredients for stuffing are spread out.

How do you know how to do all this? I ask.

Do what? Cindi sprinkles chopped-up herbs.

Cook a turkey and bake a pie.

Cindi snorts and smiles at me with the arched eyebrow she sometimes uses when I say something that shows my age. At twenty-two, I'm a few years younger but, I've deduced, eons away in life experience.

You're so funny, she tells me. Do you know how to bake a chicken? A cake? Can you even make mac and cheese? Your mom probably still does all that for you, right? Does she do your laundry, too?

I can make macaroni and cheese, I snap back. But Cindi's right. I can't cook a chicken, much less a turkey.

You need to learn how to take care of yourself, Cindi says, looking at me over her steamy eyeglasses, baster poised mid-air. No one's going to look out for you your whole life, that's for shit sure. You need to get on with it.

I look into my wine glass.

Here, mix this up with some thyme and a splash of wine, she tells me, handing over a stick of cold butter. It's hard as a rock, and I just look at it. Cindi shakes her head at me. Stick it in the microwave for a few seconds, babe.

Right.

While the turkey starts to roast, I look around Cindi's place. The furniture is minimal, but the worn couch has a hand-knit afghan folded over the back. Fashion magazines are stacked on the trunk being used as a coffee table; a couple of bras in Caribbean colors are hanging out to dry.

My family, she says, handing me a framed photo of herself in shorts and a tank top flanked by two large men in white tank tops and ball caps. They are standing together in front of a river. My brother and my dad, Cindi explains. We go to the Russian River every summer.

Who's this? I ask, picking up a photo of a dark-haired man in a navy T and aviator sunglasses. He's leaning against a stone wall, tanned arms crossed, grinning widely at the photographer.

That's Michael, my friend from L.A. He's a cop down there, a narc, Cindi says.

Are you guys, like, special friends or something? I ask, making quotation marks in the air with my fingers.

I wonder about Cindi's desires for relationships. So far from the stories she's told me, she likes fuzzy one-night stands with guys she meets in bars. While my entire existence is proscribed, static, Cindi's has a frantic, unplanned aspect to it that both alarms and fascinates me.

We're just friends, she says, wiping the photo frame glass with her apron and setting it back on the small fireplace mantle. He's the best, but we'd be horrible together. He says I need to take care of myself more, clean up my shit. He's right. Actually, you kind of sound like him sometimes.

I wander back to the kitchen. It's cozy in the warm, small space. The mushroomy smell of gravy makes my tongue water. I watch Cindi move from the fridge to the oven in her apron, humming to herself, assembling what I've now realized is probably going to be the best home-cooked meal I've had in months. Out the window, rain spits against the concrete buildings. I think of the strangeness of being here, a Canadian on American Thanksgiving, making my family meal with a girl I hardly know, a domestic goddess who dances drunk on tables and seems to see right into me.

I'm going to make you a recipe box, she announces.

What?

A recipe box. Like mine. She touches a small pine box with a hinged lid on the counter.

Roasted chicken with cream sauce, kick-ass meatloaf, my Granny's shortbread. Whenever the hell you do finally get out on your own, you're going need it. Trust me, she says.

After dinner, we watch TV and then crash for the night. In the morning I shower for a long time in her bathroom, letting the steam swirl around my head and imagining what it would be like to have my own bathroom, my own tiny apartment like this, my own tiny life.

How will I feed myself?

A couple of weeks after Thanksgiving Cindi hands me a wood box. Under the hinged lid dozens of white cards are lined up, filed by type of dish—Appetizers, Main Courses, Holiday Delights, Soups and Salads, Desserts. I flip through the cards and run my finger across the recipes, all copied out by hand in slightly slanted script.

I read through each index card, Broiled Shrimp to Yam Casserole, forward and back, then pull the whole stack of them out and search the rest of the box. I'm looking for additional instructions, something beyond "mix until all ingredients are combined and bake at 350º"; some secret message that can tell me how to do the rest of what I need to do. But that's it; there's nothing more in here.

Who will look out for me now?

At twenty-two I don't know how to become a woman who is my mother and also not my mother. This whole time she has been here, in the background, trying to make her own life in California, her back sore from receptionist chairs, helping me, trying to rear up from her own disappointment, the reality of the myth, of things not panning out. Her body, like mine, has absorbed these molecules of sun and ocean and survival, has mingled these molecules with those already circulating in her body since before either of us were born, the cells formed from the snow and forests and cities and villages and ships, cells replicated in longing and dreaming of California since it was the romantic rumor of an island the believers could not let go of. I see there is sadness in her body, and I wonder if that sadness has been invited and by whom—is this what women's bodies are fated to bring? If I listen to my body, if I follow my desires, will it leave me sad, too?

And yet

Something sits on top of the sadness, making space for something else. One night a few months before I leave I hear my mother yelling hysterically from outside the front door of the townhome complex we live in now. Oh my god! Oh my god! she screams.

What, what, I cry, panicked there is a heart attack, an intruder. I see my mother is shaking as she comes through the door, frothy with excitement, not fear.

A penis, she cries, her bleached hair sticking out every which way, our poodle Brandy at her feet crunching a tiny dog treat with his vampire teeth. I saw a penis in the bushes! Hurry up, put your shoes on, find a flashlight. You have to come with me, you have to! She waves her hands frantically in the air and I can tell she is ready for whatever is going to come next—the 911 call, the police cars and television news teams, the CNN interviews and our five minutes of fame as the closest witnesses to a Lorena Bobbitt-level scandal.

I take a flashlight from the drawer and hold my mother's hand. I am surprisingly calm. Take me to it, I tell her.

We walk outside and follow the pathway through the complex. Around a bend not far from our stall in the carport, she stops and points.

I shine the light and there it is, flesh colored, curled, lying half-cocked in the underbrush of some holly-looking plant. My mother opens her mouth but this time all that comes out is a kind of squawk. We kneel, peering deep into the greenery until I grab a stick from the ground nearby and start nudging.

Far from rigor-mortis stiff, it jiggles in its supposed life-like rubberiness, not a live penis after all but a convincing imitation, we both realize as I roll it out from under the bush. Maybe it was tossed by some scorned lover or teenager or maybe a disgusted housecleaner. My mother's hysterics explode and quickly contagion their way to me and now we are both laughing, grabbing each other's arms, bending over, shrieking, and wiping tears from our eyes. We crouch over the dildo. Should we just leave it here in the center of the walkway for the next unsuspecting person to trip over on their way home from buying groceries at Safeway? In the end we decide that would be funniest and laugh-cry our way back inside, leaving the lost penis to find its own way.

Where will I be from?

When I graduate from college with a journalism degree, out of the blue, my father arrives. Suddenly it is like all these years of separateness, of us almost never speaking, have not passed. The embarrassment, the devastation, its silencing, is swept away somewhere. It's May, I've just turned twenty-three. It took me six years to get through, but I don't care. A bluebird sky frames the snapshot of us, him in a beige sport coat, his arm around me in my royal purple graduation gown and a lei of lilies he buys me. As though my breaking away and setting out into my own life is the switch that had to be flipped for him to appear.

During this visit my parents get along. My grandparents are here too, and we celebrate my crossing a threshold by eating at a fancy restaurant. Then my father comes to our house and walks into my bedroom, where I have assembled moving boxes.

I am great at packing, he says, did you know that about me? He works swiftly, organizing items, layering boxes, pulling books and objects right off the shelves of this room he has never seen before. He is very concerned about the apartment I have rented in Palm Springs, 450 miles south, where I have accepted a job as a newspaper reporter covering government and immigration, because there is a sliding glass door in the bedroom that opens right onto the parking lot and street. We are buying you an extra lock for that door, he says, an edge to his voice. A lock and a bar. You wedge the bar along the bottom of the track and no one will be able to pry it open, he says. We're getting you one of those. An alarm maybe, too. Then he finishes the boxes, taping them tight. Packing, he says, is one of my talents.

What comes next?

She is not sure if she thinks of growing up as a beginning, or as beginning again. Beginning is, in a way, comforting; it means everything that comes before is just the prologue. The groundwork. Something to get you situated, but not the life itself. But beginning again, that to her seems more real. It allows a state of revision, an opportunity to respond to what has come before and to reorient. To correct the record. If our childhood truths were really fictions, to begin again all we must do to grow up is make more space for myth.

What do we take with us?

My father packs my boxes, and my mother buys me a wooden chest, which I fill with all the most important things until the hinged lid will barely close: pictures of my family when I was small, letters from Jason, the shark report Suzanne and I did in the sixth grade, my dolls and teddy bears, sweaters knit by my grandmother, Christmas cards from Jim, my journals and notebooks. I take all this with me and I promise myself that I will try to pack away my fear, too, the silence that filled the spaces between the things.

How does desire finish?

In the end of San Francisco, outside the theater of my mind, after my feature stories and movie reviews are filed and edited by you and you find a new girlfriend and get her pregnant and start looking for wedding venues, after the credits roll, I can't have you. When the time came I missed my lines and that is it. I have to settle for the state herself, my substitute lover who gathers me in deeply to the tribe of her, a coterie of ghostly characters who float around these borderlands, a psychic orgy of Californian kin who did or didn't get what and who they wanted but regardless possess a place for all eternity among the very real dripping eucalyptus and wet sand and palms. I am left with the specters of my desires, the things not really, and that is all I have in truth, all that goes before the aperture. Every day as I gulp down my last moments in the city I want both to run away somewhere new and to throw myself in the middle of her streets, right down there where the trolleys clang, and beg her one more time, fill me, fill me, someone please just fill me.

What will I do?

When you are twenty-three this is what you can do. You can drive all night to a job interview down a long, dark coast. To your right is the vast ocean, to your left inky fields of garlic and artichoke. You can move from San Francisco to the desert, from the cool breast of a state to the dry soles of its feet. You will be on your own for the first time, though you have felt lonely for years.

You have gone to school, gotten a degree like you were supposed to, written papers and served coffee and mopped floors, offered your body to some men and all the while investigated your desires closely enough that now you have come to know something about them. But you still have no idea what you are doing. You are afraid of where you're going and what you will find. What if you find nothing?

To keep you company on the road, and to stay awake, you spin the radio dial. Some station out of somewhere comes in, playing a song you remember but haven't heard for a long while, and suddenly you *love a rainy night.*

You roll down the window, let the moist in and the music out. For a few minutes you are five again: thick pigtails, marrying Barbie to Ken, waking up early to sneak an episode of *Twilight Zone,* everywhere you turn the safe boundaries of the mother-father-you triangle, that Eden, that far, far place.

How we say goodbye

I drive by Jim's house early on the morning I leave. I don't know if he's home. I don't get out of my car, just stop a few yards away and look for a minute.

The spring grass has come in nicely, and it's all sparkly from the dew. When I first met him he had just finished a whole summer manicuring that lawn and others in order to earn money to buy the "5-Oh." I can still feel the stiff maroon leather of the Mustang's springy seats beneath me. I can smell the burning when I ground the clutch too hard trying to learn how to drive it.

The lace front curtains are drawn; this probably means his parents are away at the boat for the weekend. I peer around the side of the house toward the backyard. I roll down my window so I can hear the gurgling of the fish pond.

I see the oil stain in the driveway that Jim left while fixing my car, and the spot where I posed on the front walkway in a bright blue lace prom dress six years ago, holding his arm.

His bedroom window is cracked open. The shaggy brown carpet, the narrow bed where I left a part of myself, his cross-country trophies, the part of his heart he gave me, all occupy a corner of space in my mind.

The dampness in the air is burning quickly. The June sun already feels hot through my windshield. Soon the neighbors will be out, scrubbing their cars in the driveway, planting summer daisies and begonias, racing tricycles around the cul-de-sac. Later the barbecues will fire up, cold beers will crack.

I take my foot off the brake and roll slowly around the quiet corner like you do when you're sneaking out.

And then I'm pressing the gas, merging onto the freeway, watching the gated developments and car lots and shopping centers blur by. In an hour I'm cruising along the coast, salt whipping through my hair. I glance up into my rearview mirror, over my stacked belongings, out the little rectangular window behind me and up into the cloudless California sky, where I see my heart floating silently out of its suburban settlement, up, up, and away.

PART EIGHT

Completion

Completion

IN THIS STAGE, THE INTERROGATION IS COMPLETED AND THE
body of information collected is analyzed. As appropriate and feasible,
the interrogator may return to the previous stages to gather more information if she needs.

What comes from inside the alone

I've been sprung. I've sprung myself and now I'm going somewhere that I've heard is a perfect fit for old people, for resort-dwelling gay guys. It used to be a fit for partying spring break kids but that's old news now, the party's moved to Havasu.

Traveling across the base of my state's spine, snaking through impossibly brown, dry canyons, I panic that I am going not to my new life but to another planet, an uninhabitable one, all gray and camel-colored rock and heat mirages rising in 110 degrees. I will be more alone here than ever and what have I done? Then I see it, the patch of green, palm fronds reaching up like yellow-tipped feathers toward chalky mountains, and also grass that I know shouldn't be indulged in a water-depleted West, but I don't care. Sting is singing on the radio about rain and desert rose and with my eyes open I drive into a dream that this is where I will find something, where I will declare myself, in this oasis ahead in the cradle of the state.

What legacies were bequeathed

They are familiars from long ago. It is hard not to believe all these palm trees are for me. They are always there as a location device, to locate yourself, to anchor yourself like them: not too deeply, needing only a little water, shallow roots strong enough to hold on but not be taken for granted. Maybe to be brought in from somewhere else but then to make yourself belong. To lodge firmly in a loamy base. To be comfortable in sands that shift and blow. To be here for now. To be here.

What is this California?

Desert is sharp angles and softly rippled dunes.
Desert is a secret between myself and myself.
Desert is the contour of exoticism.
Desert is ordinary apocalypse.
Desert is a form of liberation.
Desert is scorched hideout.
Desert is a heart storm.
Desert is a fault line.

Desert is a scouring.

Begin again

Everything dry is scorched. Scoured.

In the desert I am dry-cleansed to the bone. Bones picked clean. Expectations picked clean. Fear purged. In a landscape of vast silence it does not matter how silent you are. Every quiet breath you take matters. No one questions. I ask the questions now. Of others but also of myself, questions I will be asking always. For survival. It is important to the building of something.

One day soon after I arrive here I go out into the real desert, past the fancy resorts and golf courses and casinos and sidewalk cool-water misters, and I see that the sandy edges of it bleed out. The borders of this state, its boundaries, are at this end dissipated, the brink blown to the wind. The borders emit particles, like aliens and our messages to them. Messages echoing back to ourselves, to the aliens we are, I am.

The construction of a life. Think of Joshua Tree National Park, Black Rock Canyon, boulders balanced impossibly in goliath handfuls, all soft, rounded edges, piled high next to spiked Joshua bodies to construct a response to the landscape. Part of the landscape but also the answer to it. Here is what I have to say in return. See? See, we are talking to one another, sharp to smooth, bayonet to monzogranite, yucca to magma, drought saga to flash flood. I am speaking to the landscape, it is answering me. It answers everything I say.

Terry Tempest Williams calls Mary Austin's obsession with white "the soul heat."

What am I doing here?

"Unbounded by time or space, the California dream is transcendent, creating a unity, a whole, a merging of past, present, and future in the total California experience," writes historian James J. Rawls. "It's quite impossibly everything—and quite possibly nothing at all."

From the edge of the pool in my new apartment in the low pink complex at the edge of the loose blowing desert I hear a single dove cooing incessantly. It coos and it waits for a response.

Interrogation is a scaffold that stretches back into ancestry

November 24, 1942

KUIBYSHEV — More than 2,000 Jews—almost the entire Jewish population remaining in Smolensk—were massacred recently in that Nazi-occupied city, according to reports brought here today by N. Krilov, who succeeded in escaping from the city and reaching one of the guerrilla bands which are active in the Smolensk area.

The Jews—mostly women, children and old men—were brought in closed trucks to Gegonovka Place, Krilov disclosed. Here they were lined up before a huge pit that had been dug beforehand, and following the usual Nazi pattern the victims were machine-gunned and dumped into the pit, dead and wounded alike, and flung over them was a shallow covering of earth.

What happened to the anger they secreted away?

A day will come when she will not live in California anymore. She will be miles north, in the suburb of a perfectly nice city rimmed by deep green forests and snow-topped mountains. One cold, bright Saturday she will round the corner in her neighborhood, setting out for the grocery store. On a street narrowed down to one lane by the cars parked on either side, a car will approach hers, head on. The other driver determined not to let her pass first, ignoring several open spots free for pulling into.

There will be no openings for her to pull aside, otherwise she gladly would. She still likes to please.

They will approach each other slowly until their hoods almost touch. She will put her minivan into park, in the middle of Mary Avenue, and think, *This is awkward.* And, *This is mildly funny.*

You need to back up! the woman will call to her out the window.

I'm not reversing onto a busy street, she will roll down the window and call back, her pulse speeding up a little bit, You have room and you should have pulled over.

Then the other woman will yell: Where the hell are you from, California? Go back where you came from!

This is all it will take. A cloud of nostalgia and terror and pride will drift in out of the clear blue sky. The memory of being speechless while wanting to speak, of a place and a voice finding each other.

She will get out of her car, slam the door, cross her arms, not ready to chuckle anymore.

I have all day, she will scream at the woman, louder than planned, enough for all the neighbors to hear. Louder, truthfully, than necessary. A rage not felt in a while, a rage and an ache and a beautiful allegiance, will surge. She will be both surprised at this rage and this ache, and not surprised.

Goddamn Californians, the woman will keep yelling (how does she know?), but the Californian won't hear it.

I'M NOT MOVING, she will shout to the bitch in the car and to the whole goddamn neighborhood, feeling warmer and better the angrier she gets. I have all day, she yells, and I'm not going anywhere.

I have already been, the Californian will think, reaching for her car door. *I have already come and gone.*

What do you have to say in your own defense?

In the desert I dream wildly, dreams I throttle through—dreams where I interview people and full conversations pour out, dreams where I'm soaring off a cliff, falling down stairs, dialing phone numbers, smoothing sand sculptures. Always, the dream where I stand, mute, in a wood and marbled courtroom.

My fixation on this repetitive flash of memory is, it turns out, ordinary. A traumatic event is not assimilated or experienced fully at the time, Cathy Caruth tells us, but only belatedly, in its repeated possession of the one who experiences it: "To be traumatized is precisely to be possessed by an image or event."

One of the most viable responses to trauma is testimony.

What will it take to mother myself?

I was three or four, in my parents' station wagon in the heavy heat of a Florida afternoon. We were on our way to see my parents' friends Janie and Roger, who had a son I loved named Garett who played detective with me. Inside my shoe, sitting in the backseat, I felt a tickle. It's nothing, said my mother when I told her. We'll be there soon.

I'm sure I whined. There's something there, I complained one more time. But she told me to wait and so like a good girl I sealed my lips and did, my tickly right foot jiggling as I pumped my calf against the seat.

As soon as we walked into the relief of swamp-cooler air at Janie and Roger's house I reminded my parents to take off my shoe. My mother bent to unbuckle the Mary Jane, slid it off my socked foot, and screamed at the top of her lungs as a three-inch-long coal-colored lizard leapt free and hurried across the floor.

What is here?

I go out and I ask people to tell me their stories. I write down these stories in my reporter's notebooks and later they are printed in ink. Stories of migrant farmworkers who slip through fences, make deals with coyote devils, pick spinach, cauliflower, broccoli, onions, grapes, dates; stories of trailer parks with live wires and bad plumbing and children at play; stories of mothers who have nothing for dinner but will offer you their last cold Pepsi and not accept no thank you for an answer; stories of wealthy septuagenarians who fight pettily over covenants, conditions, and restrictions; stories of twentysomethings who launch hot-spring spas on a shoestring in the wrong end of town; stories of tennis champions; of Hollywood's gilded age; of a grandfather in a Rolls Royce who asks me at a stoplight if I am busy later; of immigrants who push mowers and change hotel sheets and float around as invisible as ghosts; stories of anonymous activists who leave barrels of water in the desert so the deaths of those on treacherous journeys, also anonymous, might be eluded; stories of transgender women who yearn to walk down the sidewalks as themselves; stories of neighbors thankful to have seen the face of Mother Mary in the pattern of a broken window's cracks.

Say what else is here

A love that splits me like the earthquake fault that crosses this valley from the Chocolate Mountains along the centerline of the Little San Bernardino Mountains. After the shock of rupture comes the oasis.

Always revisit the ceremony of crossing over

Once, long after I leave college and move down the body of the state, I return north with Suzanne to visit a place called Beckwourth Pass, where in 1851 a ten-year-old girl who would grow up to become the first poet laureate of California, led by the legendary mountain guide and former slave James Beckwourth and followed by her family's wagon, crossed over the Sierra Nevada on the back of a pony. "There, little girl," Beckwourth told her as they crested the pass he discovered but was later not repaid for developing, "there is California! There is your kingdom." Even as the girl, named Ina Coolbrith, lurched along that immigrants' route, her gray girl's eyes took in the valley ahead, the oxen behind, the nearness of the perfect clouds, and she began in her mind to write words.

Though we drive east from Sacramento and trek close in the ice and slush of a cold March, it is hard to navigate against nature, and we cannot get all the way to Ina's place of crossing like I want to. Even today with iPhones and radios and concrete one can hit an impasse. Instead I will see Beckwourth Pass best later from the air, heading away from the state: an emerald smear, surrounded by snow, the lowest point across the Sierras through which all those years ago a person with courage and supplies and most of all desire could come through. Why do you need to see this place? Suzanne asks me, with more patience than I probably deserve, as I debate whether to install metal chains on the tires of a rental car in the spitting hail on the side of a darkening highway.

I need to see this place because I am coming closer to something. Because at some point I start to understand what it takes to cross over. You do not move across the border of someplace and instantly become. You do not just belong. You may be granted permission to cross, with a stack of papers and a stamp, if you answer their questions the right way. But to assimilate demands a push through silence. To have our voice silenced, and then to bring it back. To lose one myth and build the next.

Go back, try again. And again. Begin again.

Brimmed with the golden vintage of the sun

He appears over the cubicle wall at my desk, six foot four, longish hair curling around his neck, wide grin. His name is Lukas. He's the newspaper's environmental reporter. Do you need anything, he asks me. I tell him I think I am settling in alright. Too crunchy, I say later on the phone later to Suzanne, too granola, not for me. But soon we are having lunch together at cheap taquerias and Happy Thai, where the cantaloupe-colored iced tea is the only thing that cools me in August's 110 degrees.

He knows everything about the desert, about bighorn sheep and alluvial fans and water wars. He is an encyclopedia. One night we sit under the stars at a cantina and look up at the palms hanging over downtown, their fibrous skirts trimmed short and tidy. They're not supposed to look like that, he tells me of the skirts, which are all the fronds that have already lived and died but stay attached to the body of the tree. When they're allowed to grow, he explains, the skirts become microhabitats for beetles, bats, birds, snakes.

I try to imagine those wild canopies underneath, frantic with creatures, but my skin prickles in the heat.

Another time we sit outside his place with our feet in the hot tub. The night is perfect, like every one since I've moved to the desert: obsidian sky, eggshell moon, lime green fronds lifting in the hot breeze. We talk about books, about his childhood on a patch of Arizona land off the grid of anything modern, about my stories. I only want to be friends, I tell him. No problem, he answers casually, lifting his giant feet out of the water, pivoting onto his back, dropping his head into my lap.

He travels to Arizona for a weekend to visit a woman he met at

a wedding, a woman he is interested in because I have said I am not interested in him that way. I drive him to the airport at midnight on Friday and
make myself smile when I wave him off. Then I sit with my feet in my pool
for two days and wait, listening to the frogs croak in the dry culverts, feeling the heat in my bone, surprised at my unrest.

What am I afraid of?

California's original inhabitants, her rightful inhabitants, fashioned thatched roofs for their homes from the fronds of the native fan palm, sealing their bodies from the elements but rendering porous the boundary between the landscape and the personal.

I try to maintain the boundaries between myself and nature because I am afraid of what the open desert contains. But everything creeps and bleeds; tiny white bugs crawl across the carpet. Lizards scamper past my foot on the patio; kettles of Swainson's hawks circle above. I spot a wiggling beige coil just left of the yellow center line and nearly swerve off the road. At night I dream about the fog of San Francisco, its cool pale-blue empty. Sometimes I dream that I need to contact Jim, it's some kind of emergency, but I can't recall his number or even his last name.

I don't want to go back into the fog, although the memory of it calms me. What I want is for everything before to fall away; to open myself to the desert completely. In the desert I feel like screaming, like finally I can.

It's not enough just to live

When Lukas comes back from his visit to Arizona, we go to lunch and he tells me his weekend was not fun, that with the woman he met he didn't feel right.

What does it take to be heard?

For the newspaper I write and write and write. I go to city halls and political rallies, boat races and AIDS support groups, courtrooms and living rooms. I interview people every day. I ask them easy questions and hard ones. I try to do almost everything gently. It is their choice, mostly. The regular people, the ones who aren't paid to speak to me and answer my questions even when I need to push and probe and make demands and threaten to write "so-and-so would not return calls"—with those people I tell them I want to hear their story and others do, too. I invent my own shorthand so I can capture more of what they say. What is your name, I ask, for the record?

Some days I have to sit in my car and psych myself up. I go over my questions, think about how to reach someone who is afraid or fed up or trying to disappear. I'm twenty-three. I check the clock fifty times a day. Some days by deadline I write and file two stories, three. Every morning I pick up the newspaper and look for my name. My chest pounds. Spell your name please, I always ask them twice, striving to get it all right.

A story a day, two, three. Every week it's like I did nothing the week before, and I have to prove myself again.

One day I am sent to a meeting. The members of this meeting are local politicians, CEOs of large companies, hotels and golf courses and casinos and a transit agency that runs only on sunshine. I have my notebook and my three pens, and I find the address and enter the building and find the board room. I walk in and the members are sitting around a large oval table in sport coats and damp white shirts and belt buckles. I slip into a seat against the wall and check the clock. The man at the head of the table glances around the room. Probably can't start quite yet, he says, we're expecting a reporter from the newspaper today. I am the reporter, I offer. They turn and look at me, confused.

I AM THE REPORTER, I almost shout.

What does it mean to belong?

Thousands of years ago, in the Pleistocene, the Mohave Desert was much wetter. As the lakes dried up, they left small pools and springs behind, where the ancestors of the desert pupfish clung to life and evolved. Different pools shelter different species and subspecies, all dependent on a fragile desert ecosystem threatened in many ways. Dodging electric transmission corridors, livestock grazing, and water diversions, tiny pupfish, the males of which glow blue when ready to mate, live on for now in rare desert wetlands and palm oases.

Oases are clustered along valleys where springs trickle up through gaps in the earth's plates. These are not the refuges of a mirage, a Fata Morgana; they are real, places that smell fibrous and yellow-green, of thread-bearing petticoats in heat, places you can walk through, your hand sweating inside a larger hand.

State your name for the record

One day for a story I am writing for the newspaper I take a tour of the desert with a federal border patrol guard. His intent is to show me and the photographer I am with how challenging it is for him to battle the porousness of the U. S. border here in Imperial Valley, how complex it is to monitor the systems of walls, gates, canals, and open wilderness for migrants trying to slip through. How hard it is to track them, to *keep out aliens*, and also, the guard says as an afterthought, to keep them alive. What I ask him is: How it is to keep them alive? What I write in my notebook is: Does he know it was theirs first?

In his Jeep we bump across the blistering sand of the Colorado Desert, past the refrigerator-sized plastic tubs where citizen activists place water so that dehydrated and disoriented immigrants might be able to drink instead of die. We're all working toward the same goal, really, the agent says, swerving us by a bend in the fluorescent aqua All-American Canal, a swift-running man-made river 175 feet wide that ferries the water the West fights over, near where later the photographer and I, by ourselves, will meet a group of Mexican men, modern-day Argonauts, showering from a chemical-laden agricultural runoff pipe. In my notebook I write it down when the agent says, If you don't have permission you shouldn't be coming through here. But I know there are things we shouldn't wait for permission for.

Another day I visit a small plot of earth in a cemetery in Holtville, a holy place, where rows of plain white crosses mark the sunbaked graves of migrants who are found dead in the desert, their bodies among the blue-green creosote and barbed ocotillo, or floating in the canals and ditches. They are labeled John Doe and Jane Doe, as if they never had names, nor a language of their own. As if they came from nowhere and California, once they stepped foot in it, was all there ever was.

The opposite of erasure is inscription

Soon we are slick with sweat. While tiny lizard feet scratch along the dry rocks, the sun blazes so hot we slide loose from ourselves making love.

I become an empty white heat

We drive to Mexico. We slurp sweet seafood in an empty dining room on a cliff above the Pacific. We buy tourist wine glasses and a carved stone chess set sturdy enough to last until a child not yet born is ready to learn the rules of play. We listen all night to a young couple on the other side of the hotel door fight ugly. We get sad about them then move to a quieter hotel. We lie flat under the high wood beams, our muscles like hills. We fuck against the hand-painted indigo tile. We turn each other inside out.

I know now where I want this to go

In *The Land of Little Rain*, published in 1903, naturalist Mary Austin surfaces and interrogates several aspects of the California myth—generally understood as the at-times-foolhardy belief that California is a sort of Eden, a western paradise where, if you can get to it, all your problems will be solved and every one of life's riches is ripe for the taking. In the slender book—part travelogue, part backcountry guide, part sociological study, and part prophetic environmental warning—Austin, like other naturalist writers of the era, situates nature in its untouched form as a salve for the soul, much as some believe God is or can be. And she warns those chasing the dream to heed the lessons of the people here first.

In her introduction to a later edition of *The Land of Little Rain*, Terry Tempest Williams quotes biographer Esther Lanigan Stineman: "While many Americans turned to old cathedrals and traditions of Europe, or even the far East, to alleviate anxieties emanating from an increasingly mechanized and industrialized world, Austin found a solution in America itself." Austin's Biblical allusions position the Southwest, with its magical waters hidden in Shangri-La deserts, as a spiritual journey. A sacred place we are pulled to by powers and patterns larger than ourselves. "No man can be stronger than his destiny," Austin writes.

Like the ideal outcome of going west, *The Land of Little Rain* arcs from the Mojave Desert to the lusher lands: from want to fulfillment.

From drought to plenty.

Her intellect and heart had their home in desert places

It was not all easy. It was not all slick like seals. It was not all ear-piercing pleasure in the desert.

He was raw and I was raw but in two different ways. He did not care about anything that composed an image or an ego. He was stripped down. He liked objects that were worked over, falling-apart furniture and holey T-shirts. He was of the land, not just tiptoeing across it like I was. He danced like a drunk turkey because it made him happy. He had begun again a while back and was further ahead.

I was finding a voice, but I still worried about who was watching. Don't be, he whispered into me, you can say anything you want. He wanted to hear me scream.

We moved in together after being questioned by a Palm Springs landlord in a white pantsuit named Merle, who wanted to make sure we thought Jesus would be alright with it. We bit our lips and said we thought he would be.

We moved in together and nature moved in with us. In the shower, desert cockroaches as big as matchboxes fell on me. Bighorn sheep, their heads heavy, clicked calmly down the mountain and circled our apartment, flirting languidly with traffic until Lukas phoned the agency with Jeeps that gently chased them back up the rocks. His cat, Girlfriend, brought in birds and desert mice and other things still alive.

What does it mean to be good?

One night a few months after we moved into a desert apartment brimming with fuchsia bougainvillea, I was leaning over to switch off the light on my bedside table when I glimpsed something iridescent coral, scales like jewels, on the carpet beside me. It moved, flashing a tail. I flew upright and stood on the bed, the scream already pouring from me.

Lukas moved quickly, on hands and knees, closing doors, shuffling furniture, coaxing and trapping while I kept my eyes squeezed shut and cried, not thinking for a second to smile, to wait patiently.

It's out, he said after a few minutes, waving the lizard on its way. How big, I gasped, sinking into the pillows. A foot or two he said and grinned.

I scowled at Girlfriend, who sat still in the corner looking at us like, what?

What is at risk?

One weekend we hiked up into the gray-brown hills along a seared trail that crumbled under our boots. I was jumpy, scanning for coils of white or brown, listening for rattling, thinking ahead to a margarita with dinner, to the inside cool. Relax, he said, and I tried but also resisted, said to myself about him, Fuck you, fear is not so permeable.

We passed the remains of a long-ago cabin, only its sooted brick chimney remaining, angled sideways like a frontier Tower of Pisa. Desert rats, the locals called the type of person who came out to the empty to hide, to piece together a shack and crouch below the radar of scrutiny.

Up ahead and off the edge of the trail, in a hollow piled with small boulders and debris, sat a desiccated armchair, sun-bleached stuffing and springs popping out the center. Lukas got a look on his face and scrambled down the slope.

No! I called, loudly, Don't you even. Why not, he shrugged, pausing to look up at me, his brow a question. And he eased himself in, unconcerned about what else might be lurking or how the borders of human and landscape were growing messier all the time.

I watched him lean back, sitting there all relaxed in that desert rat chair, long abandoned to the elements, grinning at me like he had the answer to something.

What is the lesson?

The desert around Palm Springs is the only place in the world that provides habitat for the webbed-foot Coachella Valley fringe-toed lizard, special because of how it saunters, ballerina-like, across the shifting dunes. The lizard is endangered thanks to nonnative grasses. The grasses, brought by humans, take hold on the dunes and interrupt the fine windblown sand the lizard requires to live.

Too much grass, too much rooting, solidifies the dunes when they are supposed to remain moving and free.

What do I think California will be like?

In the Southern California desert the place I found that most disturbs is a body of water called the Salton Sea. The manmade sea is the largest lake in California, smack on the San Andreas Fault. When a levee broke along the Colorado River in 1905, the sea formed in its basin below sea level. Inflow came after that from agricultural runoff, started coming and couldn't stop. Evaporation is the only outflow, so salt levels in the sea have grown and grown and grown; it is 30 percent saltier than the ocean.

    In the fifties and sixties, the thirty-five-mile-long lake drew vacationers in droves. They came to the sea's luxury hotels from Los Angeles and beyond in station wagons and campers, Elvis and the Beach Boys crooning from speakers, suntan oil ready. Celebrities and the wealthy raced speedboats on the lake, the salinity offering a buoyancy that lifted the boats and a thrill that could not be matched. In the eighties, the Department of Fish and Wildlife introduced sport fishing, and hundreds of species of birds riding the Pacific Flyway, desperate for wetlands as the state's development gobbled up nature's spaces, descended on the water en masse. At one time, 400,000 boats a year bobbed on the lake. More people visited the Salton Sea than Yosemite National Park.

    But what man makes, nature eventually wrenches back. Because the lake's inflow comes mostly from agricultural runoff, nutrients and fertilizers built up. Eutrophication, it's called, excessive nutrients in a body of water. This causes algae blooms and other microscopic plants to flourish—a growth cycle that has Frankensteined: The blooms block out the sun, obstructing bottom-dwelling plants. When the algae dies it uses all the dissolved oxygen. The fish literally suffocate. Scientists have attempted many solutions to save the sea, the fish, the birds, but none have proven viable, and time is running out.

Yet despite this imminent death, the lake is one of the most ecologically fruitful places on Earth. Time here is on fast-forward, on steroids. Nutrients, warm water, and prolific species mix to make a swarming cocktail of life.

Lukas wrote often for the newspaper about the sea, its animals, and the environmental implications of its evolution. The idea of a massive lake—even a flawed one—in the midst of a thirsty desert enthralled me; I wanted to see it for myself. One Saturday we took the fifty-mile drive east from Palm Springs along Highway 111, moving out of the urban area where we lived, away from the steakhouses and multiplex theaters that had begun to creep up on the formerly sleepy strip of desert resorts and second homes, into farmland and then the desert's gaping beige empty.

After an hour we arrived at the Salton Sea and pulled into an area that had once been called Bombay Beach, a place that was now, I could see, only a burned-out backdrop for hollow trailers, abandoned motels, jagged signposts, and the remnants of pier pilings slowly overtaken by the lake's lapping, killer water. All that remained of a place that once epitomized the California dream was an arid ghost town shimmering on this desert edge of a lake that at first seemed to me so blue and sprawling and incongruous it should be a phantasm.

We left the car on the road and walked toward the sea. On approach, the shore appeared to be made of sand, like most beaches. But once we stepped onto it, I saw that the sand was not sand at all but a graveyard made entirely of crushed fish bones. Deprived of oxygen, millions of fish a year wash up dead. They are pecked at by birds, scorched by the sun, stripped and shriveled, reduced to skeleton and dust.

The water, I saw, was a deception, too. Up close, from that white shore of ashes, it was no longer cerulean but a murky brown, or in some angles of light an otherworldly yellow, glowing with warning.

I bent and scooped a handful of crushed fish, letting the pieces of carcass sift through my fingers. The air around us stank like sulfur, full with the orgasm of rot. Holding our breaths, we held hands and sunk our toes into the bones.

The myth and the mirage

I've said nothing about grief. Which means I have said nothing. Or maybe I have spoken of it, or tucked it between the silences, my own fault margins. In any case it is here, trying to stay folded and unseen, like crusts and rift zones and salt basins, stretching and sinking and rupturing, reshaped by the combined actions of the forces of time. It is in the grooves of a spinning 45. In the tip of the needle of the arm of a brushed steel turntable in a mahogany box, lifted with all the delicacy a six-year-old girl's fingers can muster. A good girl. A needle placed carefully on the record while her mother and father look on.

Where are you really from?

I will leave California one day. But, before that, I return to her, from a trip east with Lukas to his family's land in Arizona. After a few days there we drive back westward through the fields of saguaros and cholla and prickly pear his parents can turn into wine. In this expanse of nothing we have a hard fight that travels for hours and hours and rips everything open, pulling the seams apart like grains of sand. It is about assimilating into each other. To make something new you must shift your allegiance, something he is slow to realize and I am impatient to resolve.

      The desert shames us with her species' adaptations, Austin writes, their ability to flower, to fruit in the waterless scorch, to scamper and scavenge and procreate. "One hopes the land may breed like qualities in her human offspring, not tritely to 'try' but to do."

      In the white truce of noon, moving west along that open road, we speed all the way up to the crumbling, arid precipice, and then, somehow, we slowly circle ourselves back. To drink from the fabled desert river Hassaympa, Austin tells us, is to "no more see fact as naked fact, but all radiance as with the color of romance." Hollowed out from our fight, more awake than we've ever been, we seek out the quenching shade, the spring that will water us a long time.

Completion

On the other end of that fight in the middle of nowhere on the hot ribbon of the 10 we reach the dividing line between Arizona and California and, how strange, a guard in a box awaits us. Watching the border, I suppose, checking for proof and for truth.

Lukas rolls down the window to the furnace heat.

Just you two? the guard, in aviators, asks.

We nod. I look ahead of us on the road, which points all the way west to the Pacific Ocean, the blacktop flickering in the heat the same way the road behind us from Phoenix did. Just ahead, beyond this invisible border, is a different place. The map says so. This sign at the booth, Welcome to California, says so.

I look at the guard, who asks us: Where are you headed?

And here's where I do a funny thing. I don't even have being newly landed as an excuse—I've been here eight years already. But maybe it takes that long.

Where are you headed? he asks us.

From the passenger seat I lean across Lukas, my hand curved over the solid berm of his thigh, the skin whose salt I have drank.

Where am I headed?

California! I blurt, involuntarily, triumphant at my silly naming of not a city or town, which is the specific final destination the guard wants to know, but instead just the obvious name of the dirt we've already rolled onto. When ordered to explain myself, I state the place I'm clearly going.

California.

Here is my moment of crossing, the evidence of it. Of being absorbed.

Acknowledgments

I AM IMMENSELY GRATEFUL TO THE EDITORIAL STAFF AT HAWTHORNE Books, particularly Rhonda Hughes, who saw my California dream the way I hoped it could be seen. Thanks to Sarah Dowling for the many patient reads and encouragement, and to the faculty and my cohort at the University of Washington Bothell MFA in Creative Writing and Poetics (especially Dave Sanders, Tracy Gregory, Ellen Donnelly, Andrew Carson, Rebecca Brown, Jeanne Heuving, and Amaranth Borsuk) for receiving and responding to my work. Endless gratitude to Kellini Walter, Dana Montanari, Wendy Staley Colbert, and Abigail Carter for your support, love, words, breakfasts, escapes to cozy cabins with wood-burning stoves, and for traveling this writer journey alongside me. Special thank you to Theo Nestor, for showing me how it's done and for providing unconditional reassurance, inspiration, and, when needed, life support, and for your more-precious-than-gold friendship. To Suzanne Swirsky, my lifelong champion, shark expert, memory holder, the Diana Barry to my Anne Shirley: I would be nothing without you. My deepest love and gratitude to Lukas, Lola, and Tansy Velush, who form the shape of my heart. And to my family, and especially to my parents: thank you for the music.